COMMUNICATION RESEARCH FOR DEVELOPMENT

The ISRO Experience

About the Editors

Binod C. Agrawal (Ph. D. Wisconsin) is responsible for conducting social impact studies of various programmes of ISRO. He taught at Iowa State University and at the Indian Agricultural Research Institute, Delhi. He has several publications- books and papers in international journals - to his credit. Dr. Agrawal organized the X International Congress of Anthropological and Ethnological Science (1978) and is responsible for organizing the 15th International Association of Mass Communication Research General Assembly and Conference (1986).

S.R. Joshi has Master's degree in psychology and he is working in the field of television research for more than eight years. He has specialized in the area of formative research and participated in international courses in India and abroad. He also worked on a UNESCO project. Mr. Joshi's special interest area is television and women. He is attached to Kheda Communication project of DECU, ISRO.

Arbind Sinha (Ph. D. Vik) is one of the few scholars who continues to work in the field of communication since the days of Satellite Instructional Television Experiment. He contributed papers in several national and international journals. His publications include Mass Media and Rural Development (1985) and SITE to INSAT (1986). He organized sessions in X International Congress of Anthropological and Ethological Science (India, 1978) and the XI Congress (Canada, 1983). Dr. Sinha has also established himself in the field of disaster communication.

COMMUNICATION RESEARCH FOR DEVELOPMENT

The ISRO Experience

Edited by
Binod C. Agrawal
S.R. Joshi
Arbind Sinha

Published for

Development and Educational Communication Unit
Indian Space Research Organisation, Ahmedabad

by

CONCEPT PUBLISHING COMPANY PVT. LTD.
NEW DELHI-110059

ISBN : 978-81-7022-073-2

Edition 2019

Published and Printed by

Concept Publishing Company Pvt. Ltd.
A/15-16, Commercial Block, Mohan Garden,
New Delhi-110059 (INDIA)
T : +91 11 25351460, +91 11 25351794
E : publishing@conceptpub.com, *W* : www.conceptpub.com

Cataloging in Publication Data--Courtesy: D.K. Agencies (P) Ltd. <docinfo@dkagencies.com>

Communication research for development : the ISRO experience / edited by Binod C. Agrawal, S.R. Joshi and Arbind Sinha.

pages cm

Reprint. Originally published: 1986.
Includes bibliographical references and index.
ISBN 9788170220732

1. Television in community development--India. 2. Television and women--India. 3. Television and youth--India. 4. Artificial satellites in telecommunication--India. I. Agrawal, Binod C., 1942- editor. II. Joshi, Subhash R., 1944- editor. III. Sinha, Arbind K., editor. IV. Indian Space Research Organisation. Development and Educational Communication Unit.

LCC HN690.Z9C6 2019 | DDC 307.140954 23

PREFACE

In 1973, we started planning and designing for Social Research and Evaluation of Satellite Instructional Television Experiment (SITE). This project was responsible for the creation of "Communication Research Group" within Development and Educational Communication Unit, Indian Space Research Organisation, Ahmedabad. The researchers who worked on SITE opened up new vistas for communication research, specially television. "Several anthropology departments have started offering 'Communication Anthropology', a number of sociology departments have produced M.Phil and Ph.D. level thesis, extension education departments along with child development departments have started discussing the use of educational technology, particularly television for imparting skill and knowledge to young children and students".

It is in this kind of communication environment within the country that ISRO researchers have made modest contributions which have been reflected in the papers presented in this volume.

In 1973, the terms 'Audience Profile' and 'Need Assessment Studies' were quite foreign to several of us. Even the term pretesting of a 'television programme' was only occasionally heard. Today these are accepted terms in our vocabulary and formative research has matured within the communication research field in India. We take genuine pride in initiating formative research within India. The value of communication research and evaluation as an integral element in television production for planning decisions and mid-core corrections is no more questionable. Major television serials, development programmes and programmes meant for higher education are now being pretested. Still one wonders as to what extent have we been in a position to prove our worth as communication researchers in academics and media organisations? Have we been able to create jobs only for researchers in media organisations or in addition, have we been able to make meaningful contributions? While Agrawal's paper provides a historical perspective, Joshi and Joshi & Trivedi's papers indicate the actual application of research in television production. Trivedi's paper argues for researchers to take catalystic roles in introducing social change.

In many ways this enlarges the scope for communication researchers.

In this volume, our attempt is to privide review research papers related to two major communication projects undertaken by ISRO. The first project is Satellite Instructional Television Experiment (SITE) conducted in 1975-76 and second Kheda Communication Project (KCP) is running into eleventh year.

We take this opportunity to thank Mr K S Karnik, Director, Development and Educational Communciation Unit (DECU), who encouraged us to bring out this volume and provided all supports required for it. Ms Radhika Mullick provided us editorial assistance and we thankfully acknowledge her help. We are also thankful to Mrs. Omana Raghavan for typing the manuscript. Credit for bringing art the book within 100 hours goes to the publisher—The Concept Publishing Company.

Ahmedabad
August 22, 1986

Editors

CONTENTS

Binod C. Agrawal

SITE COMMUNICATION RESEARCH : A REVIEW

The aim of this review paper is to present an analysis of the communication research tradition(s) that have emerged due to Satellite Instructional Television Experiment (SITE) conducted for a year during 1975-76. It will be presented in three parts. In the first part, all the 'before SITE' research efforts meant to help define and formulate the design of the experiment, production strategy and logistics of community television operation will be presented. In the second part 'SITE research' will be discussed. In the third part, 'SITE continuity' research will be described briefly. While discussing SITE research, it should be clearly understood that the term research in the present context refers to "social research" or "software" that was conducted as a part of SITE Social Evaluation. Such a clarification is considered necessary as engineers have also conducted, if not more, equally important researches related to SITE. Broadly SITE research in each part will be discussed under three sub-headings. These are (a) formative (b) process and (c) summative although earlier I have discussed it under five sub-headings (Agrawal 1981a). In addition, I will touch upon the SITE management research - an aspect little known but of immense importance and implications for communication researchers.

Three social science research traditions namely Anthropology, Sociology and Psychology significantly influenced the research on SITE. Each discipline's theoretical and methodological preoccupations are reflected in the SITE research. In almost every available SITE research document, it has been asserted that SITE research "was conceived as **inter** and **multi** disciplinary involving many disciplines of social sciences" (Agrawal 1976a; 1977b). However, while it is true that a multi-disciplinary approach was followed in SITE, the same cannot be said about an inter-disciplinary approach.

Table 1 provides a representation of the inter-linkages of disciplines, types of research and time periods of SITE research. The figure does not indicate a separate category for management and other researches which will be examined in the end while discussing research trends.

Table 1 : Showing Research Discipline, Types and Time Periods.

			Anthropology
Disciplines		Psychology	
	Sociology		
Type of Research	Before SITE (1967-73)	SITE (1973-77)	SITE Continuity (1977-)
Formative	No	Yes	Yes
Process	Yes	Yes	Yes
Summative	Yes	Yes	?

~~to be pasted on p 24~~

The scope of research categories used here must be defined in order to understand their contextual meaning and also to have a broader perspective on these categories.

The Research Categories

The term formative research in the present context refers to a set of studies undertaken prior to planning and execution of production decisions. In education, it involves the collection of appropriate data during the construction and testing of a new curriculum in such a way that revisions of the curriculum can be done on the basis of this evidence. In the context of television, formative research was strongly advocated by the makers of Ceasame Street in Children's Television Workshop. According to Palmer (1976:96), "First, important objectives are clearly identified, then systematic audience tests are carried out in order to evaluate progress toward their achievement during the actual course of a programme production. Formative research is typically contrasted with summative research which is concerned with follow-up testing to determine the educational effect of new products and practices when actually put into use". In SITE, a similar methodological approach of formative research was followed. The basic assumption was that the research production collaboration will help define the goals of the programme to improve the technical content and quality of production (Aghi 1977a).

The other kinds of formative research included audience

profile and need assessment studies. Both these studies were conducted to know the characteristics of the rural audience and their needs (Agrawal 1981a).

Process research differs from formative research as it focuses on feed-back studies to analyse the viewer's reaction (Bhaskaran 1976). Content analysis of TV programmes is done to correlate and compare between intention and impact. In case of SITE, Process research also involved researches related to TV operation and other related problems of community viewing.

Summative research includes impact or effect evaluations of television on the viewers. In SITE, various kinds of studies were conducted; on measuring the effects of morning TV on school children, primary school teachers, on extension workers and farmers of Andhra Pradesh and Karnataka[1] and adult evening viewers (Agrawal 1976a). The three researches were carried out before SITE i.e. at the pre-SITE stage, during SITE and also after SITE.

Pre-SITE Research

Krishi Darshan (a programme for farmers) was initiated as a pilot project of SITE on January 26, 1967. In this pilot project out of some 300 villages of Delhi territory, 80 villages were provided with community TV sets. The selection of villages was based on the criteria of distance and availability of electricity in the village. Accordingly, the villages located within the radius of 35 kilometers from the transmitter centre, Delhi, with electricity were selected for the pilot project.

Twice a week in the evening, special programmes for farmers were telecast to provide latest information on farm technology. Later the frequency was increased to thrice a week.

Pre-SITE, research falls into process and summative categories. Between 1967 and 1972 a series of feedback and impact studies were conducted to measure the effects of Krishi Darshan. The basic assumption in all these has been that external knowledge provided through TV will change the attitude and knowledge of the farmers and will help in the adoption of agricultural innovations. The most important theoretical postulation that has influenced all these studies is the five stage "adoption process" model (Rogers 1962). Even after the publication of several articles and books rejecting the five stage process of adoption and the revision of this theoretical postulate by the author, Krishi Darshan related researches followed the same model for subsequent studies.

Without exception, Krishi Darshan researches followed the survey approach. In most studies 'before' and 'after' experimental research design was also followed for evaluating the effectiveness of TV in imparting knowledge about agricultural innovations to the farmers. Few feedback studies were part of summative evaluation. In addition, efforts were made to collect feedback data with the help of convenors of community TV.

Process Research

Krishi Darshan Continues: Krish Darshan evaluation provided programme specific feedback for action. The data were collected with the help of a schedule which included items like "programme preference", "information gain", "usefulness of information", and "discussion after viewing". In addition, general remarks of the farmers were noted. The researchers also investigated the organizational aspects of community viewing and TV operation and maintenance. Another method of continuous feedback was designed in which the TV convenor in each village was asked to provide information about TV operation, post telecast discussion through a mail feedback questionnaire. This method of data collection did not yield more than 17 per cent of the total feedback replies (Lal 1971). Another effort was to complete all the questions. It is not known how far these analyses help to improve Krishi Darshan programmes (Lal 1970).

Outside, Extension Departments of Delhi, Department of Adult Education then under National Council of Educational Research and Training (NCERT), New Delhi took the formal responsibility to evaluate Krishi Darshan. The researchers of NCERT responsible for adult education thought that Krishi Darshan television meant only for "informal education" of the farmers.

Accordingly, they raised among their questions: "How far is TV actually effective in terms of helping farmers to learn about the improved agricultural practices and making their attitude favourable towards adoption of agricultural innovations? Do farmers gain more knowledge by seeing television, and to what extent and how long do they retain the knowledge gain?" (Anonymous 1969:1).

There are two interesting faatures emerging from these studies. One, NCERT in its experimental research design took a sample of 120 respondents in the experimental group whereas the control group consisted of only 60 respondents. The studies were confined to Krishi Darshan programmes and no efforts were made to know how other programmes were viewed in the community viewing situation.

Other studies as a part of 'before SITE' research included an evaluation to measure the **Impact of Film on Indian Society** (nd). This study was sponsored by Indian Space Research Organisation in which the history of the Indian film was traced and box-office hits were content analysed in order to get insights into the nature of the film medium (Anonymous nd). In addition, a survey was conducted in two towns of Maharashtra to explore the possible effects of cinema viewing on youth. The researches hoped that the study would help in defining SITE production formats. During the same period another effort was made to outline the possible uses of satellite communication for family planning and to focus attention of inter-disciplinary view-points on problems of developmental communication. Several general articles on SITE appeared in this period but mostly as views on SITE.

SITE Configuration

SITE was one of the biggest, technologically most advanced "techno-social" experiment in direct broadcasting for education and development. "In this experiment the experimenters' main objective was to provide instantaneous information for national development to those who otherwise would have been deprived of such information for many years to come due to technological constraints" (Agrawal 1978: 1). "The basic rural educational and developmental goals of SITE were to improve general primary school education, provide teachers training, help improve agricultural practices, health and hygiene, nutrition, and contribute to family planning and national integration" (Agrawal 1981: b).

SITE was conducted in 2330 villages spanning 20 districts of economically backward States namely Andhra Pradesh, Bihar, Karnataka, Madhya Pradesh, Orissa, Rajasthan and Kheda district of Gujarat. In each village, except Kheda, a direct reception system (DRS) television was installed in a public place for community viewing. In Kheda, approximately 504 conventional 61 cm TV sets in 335 villages were installed which received the satellite TV signals through a rediffusion system. The Kheda TV remained operational after SITE. The target TV viewers of SITE were broadly divided into two categories - adults and school going primary school children, in the age group of 5-12 years. In addition, special target viewers included primary school teachers, village level workers and other agriculture development functionaries.

For adult viewers, the TV programmes were telecast in the evening for about two and half hours in which half hour was devoted to common national programme in Hindi language. The remaining two hours telecast time was equally divided for six States in four languages whereas Kheda had half hour Gujarati and half hour common national programme. For school children, the TV programmes were telecast in the morning for 22 1/2 minutes in four languages. During holidays, morning TV time was utilised for training.

SITE Research

SITE research followed a conceptual frame which is described in Table 1. The three research traditions of anthropology, sociology and psychology were followed in SITE research.

Anthropological Tradition

In recent years there is a growing realisation that anthropological methods and techniques are useful in communication research and evaluation. This is more so in the Third world countries where media and related communication researches arrived fairly late. In the case of SITE research the involvement of anthropologists was no accident as several social scientists suggested that qualitative descriptive evaluations in addition to sample surveys should be conducted to evaluate the effects of satellite TV on maiden rural viewers.

Formative Research

Formative research was conducted for a period of about 20 months before SITE. The central concern of formative research was to know the rural TV viewers, their needs and provide research support to improve the technical content and quality of television production, keeping in view the target TV viewers and the objective of the programmes.

Audience Profile: With the help of Benedict's (1934) configurational approach the audience profiles of the SITE clusters were prepared. Around the configuration the total culture was portrayed giving a psycho-cultural picture which was needed to help producers know their TV viewers. For example, Madhya Pradesh SITE area consisted of four districts namely Raipur, Durg, Rajnandgaon and Bilaspur. It was observed that the numerically dominant women enjoyed a higher status as compared to men. Careful observation and analysis of primary ethnographic data collected from 15 villages and existing literature led to the development of a "women dominated-rice-eating" configuration. Broadly social structure and organisation, occupational pattern, material culture and infrastructure facilities of these villages were described.

Trained Anthropologists in the field tended to study known ethnographic categories and in many cases just could not move out of their rigid disciplinary boundaries. The upshot was uneven descriptive analysis in time and space. Also photographs which were essential for the visual understanding of rural life could not be incorporated in these profiles. One of the serious lacunae was lack of any description on children who constituted large majority of the TV viewers.

Need Assessment: Goodenough (1963) identified three kinds of needs. These are "felt needs", "observed needs" and "real needs". The felt needs are those which are expressed by the target group whereas observed needs are those which are perceived by the change agent of education and development. Neither should be confused with real needs which can be assessed only after finding out the first two needs. Since it seemed difficult to assess the felt needs of the target TV viewers through their verbal response, only the observed needs were assessed. The need assessment studies were conducted in all the six States and Kheda district.

Indepth interviews with the help of a 15 item schedule of district, block and village level development officials provided the primary data for this purpose. On an average about 75 such officials were interviewed in each SITE State. However, later the authors of these studies felt that the assessment of felt needs would have been far more useful than observed needs.

Programme Pre-test: Eventhough few pre-test studies of television programmes were undertaken by anthropologists, they did not have any theoretical or conceptual support from their discipline for this kind of reasearch. However, the idea of participant observation and the **emic** approach to provide contextual analysis were found useful to the producers. Psychological methods and techniques were also used for pre-testing TV programmes to improve their quality and content. Extensively the science education programmes meant for school children were pre-tested both in the studio and village situations.

In the formative research the effort was to test the script before its production the assumption being that it would lead to better production, hence better impact at a lower cost to achieve the educational goal. It would not be out of place to mention that this was the first time in India that any formative research was conducted on such a scale. These pre-testing, later termed "quick and dirty" research were very useful to the producers. The most important outcome of the SITE formative research was the beginning of "team mode of TV production". The team in this case generally consisted of three sets of professionals, the producer, researcher, and the subject specialist. This part of SITE research became the basis for SITE Continuity Research in the SITE Continuity Phase.

Process Research

In SITE, process research occupied an important place especially to provide continuous and regular feedback to the production system (in this case Doordarshan). It was conducted in western communication research tradition of programme rating. Process research included among other things (a) assessment of viewers response to TV programmes in terms of comprehension, credibility, and utility, viewers size and its composition, and several such variables from among the related panel of TV villages; (b) estimation of working of community TV at any given time and other social aspects of community TV viewing and (c) content analysis of the TV messages.

Feedback

SITE feedback research was of its own kind in which field investigators lived in the SITE selected villages and collected data every day. The study provided ratings of the TV programmes in pre-determined categories. A very elaborate management structure was required to collect and analyse the feedback from 112 panel villages of six States and Kheda. Data was collected regularly for the morning and evening transmission separately. Each research assistant visited one village a day on rotation basis. In this way regular feedback data were collected from 28 villages every evening. And in the morning too, when the schools were open. While evening data were collected both in the night and on the following morning from the adult viewers, the morning data from the school children were collected just after the telecast in the school. Data were also collected from the teachers regarding the opinion on the utility of the TV programmes, their attitude towards TV and their participation in the programme. Although methodologically a very sound research design was executed, the reports of the study did not find favour with the ultimate users - the producers. Modifications were made in the method of data collection from quantitative to qualitative but very little use of the findings was made in terms of influencing the Doordarshan production methods and techniques.

As indicated earlier, before SITE, feedback data were collected with the help of the TV convenors who were expected to fill the feedback questionnaire and mail it to the convenors. In SITE, a similar but more elaborate method of feedback data on the TV operation and viewers size was attempted. The TV operation study was undertaken with the help of custodians. In a pre-paid monthly post card the TV operation custodian of each village was expected to send information on TV (Bhatia 1977a and Ahamed 1977). Also each custodian was provided a pre-coded Attendance Register for collecting viewing data. These data were collected and computerised but they were found unuseable due to low reliability of the data. It would be advisable to give very serious thought to this issue as such informations are required for decision making. So far, an appropriate method for feedback has not been evolved especially in the cultural context of India.

In future, research innovations are required to evolve better feedback research designs applicable to rural/urban Indian situation and meaningful for the producers, decision makers, and policy makers.

Content analysis of SITE programmes was conducted in order to analyse the kinds of thoughts that were conveyed to the rural viewers. So, a sample of SITE programme was content analysed (Mody 1977, 1979). This was considered as an indirect but systematic method for observing and analysing expressed communication behaviour. TV programmes, both meant for school children and adults, on a sample basis, were analysed. The method of analysis was based on the American communication research tradition. This study was to help understand the links between the message, the message makers and the message receivers. However, the content anlysis study remained unused by other researchers though it provided broad understanding of the programming over the whole year of SITE and several insights about the production constraints. It would be essential to develop methods and techniques of content analysis in the Indian cultural context. Such an analysis will provide possible indirect effects of TV on both national and regional languages and linguistic behaviour.

Summative Research

Given the nature of anthropological field work the process and summative researches of SITE were conducted together.

Hence, both have been discussed together.

Intensive field work using holistic approach in a comparative perspective to understand the process of TV communication within the cultural context was thought to have three distinct methodological advantages in providing (a) intensive first hand data (b) a great deal of indepth and intimate understanding of the process of communication and change and (c) descriptive analysis of the socio-cultural reality depicted as a whole - the whole being a SITE village (Agrawal 1981a).

The methodological issues involved the problem of selecting a "typical village" from each SITE State for this purpose and defining the scope and duration of the field study the question of incorporating the elements of experimentation and evaluation in such a study.

One of the main criticisms of the holistic study offered by Gore (1979:184) that "the researches seem to have followed the routine pattern of ethnographic reporting..." valid especially when no such use of anthropological tradition was known to the anthropologists who worked on SITE research. Nine village studies and one special study on women was conducted in this category of study (see Agrawal 1978a).

So far I have discussed as to how the anthropological method was utilised in SITE research at various levels and contexts. The theoretical and the methodological basis for using such a method in communication research, I think must be discussed in the country specific context, keeping in view the historical development of communication research **vis-a-vis** other social sciences and research tools free from being "culture specific" and allowing deeper probing and understanding of communication process. The anthropological method for communication research found favour in the Indian context because of the disenchantment with the quantitative 'impact' or 'effect' sample survey and at the same time its suitability in village and tribal India.

The psychological methods and techniques were used to measure the impact of viewing on the school children. Broadly the study design consisted of experimental design of experimental (SITE) and control (non-SITE) school children of III and V grade. Comparable instruments in different languages were prepared to test for language development. Test of achievement was also prepared for grade III and V. For classroom interaction of teachers and students, Flander's interaction-analysis system was used. Some data from grade I was also collected in post-SITE period. All these instruments were developed to suit Indian rural condition (Shukla and Kumar 1977). Similar but smaller studies were also conducted by Aghi (1977a and b) and Rahman (nd) and few others. In these studies broadly an experimental research design was followed. No such study is available after SITE to compare whether it can be applied in other rural areas.

Large scale sample survey in the sociological tradition was conducted to measure the impact of SITE on adults. The major studies of this tradition that are available today are those of Agrawal **el. al** (1977), Planning Commission (nd) and a series of small studies conducted in a single State (Chauhan and Sinha 1976, 1977 and 1979, Dighe and Roy 1977, Doshi 1978, Eapen 1979, Ramadasmorthy and Rao, 1978, and Trehan 1979).

In all these studies an experimental design of one kind or the other was used for measuring the impact of SITE on adults in some specific instructional area(s). Theoretically all the researches assumed that the information provided through television would go through a process of research design as done in before-SITE studies. Two major deviations in the research design generally observed relate to unequal control and experimental sample sizes, and additional observation during SITE in addition to pre and post observations. What are some of its methodological implications? No serious discussions have taken place among the social scientists on these issues. However, it would not be out of place to indicate that a similar research design was followed in "before SITE" survey. In a community viewing situation where TV was to be introduced for the first time, it was not possible to define viewers prior to experimentation. Hence, a larger experimental sample helped in getting a sub-sample of viewers at the time of analysis for comparision with the control group. Another serious question raised about the impact survey relates to the appropriateness of method of data collection. The investigators in the field reported time and again about the difficulty of the respondents in answering "close ended" questions. It was more so among the women respondents. To keep an individual interview "confidential" was found most difficult throughtout the survey. At best, sometime these interviews were "group interviews" and not an individual response. These observations are not new and are known to the researchers. But at the same time these difficulties should be brought out in order to understand the nature and quality of survey data.

Management and Utilization Research

In the original plan of SITE no mention was made about SITE management utilization research. However, as SITE work progressed the managers working on the project became keenly aware about the importance of such researches for future project management and optimal use of television in education and development. Accordingly, two types of studies were conducted. These are utilization and management studies. To evaluate the extent to which TV was utilized by the farmers during SITE, a study was carried out by Bhatia and Chauhan (1977). They tried to measure the effectiveness of utilization. Efforts mounted in the experiment postulated that there were three important elements interacting in the developmental process at the village level. These were the farmer, the extension agencies and mass media (Television in the case of SITE). Television provided information which was followed up and reinforced by the extension agencies leading to increase in knowledge of the farmer, subsequent change in attitude and hebaviour (Bhatia and Chauhan, 1977). They adopted "Solomon four" type of experimental design to measure the effects. They preferred this design as it enables the analysis of interaction effects or Hawthorne effect. A similar study of media utilization was conduted in Andhra Pradesh and Karnataka (Sanjay, 1977).

In the field of management, a number of professional managers who worked on the SITE wrote their personal experiences and also conducted analytical studies using case study approach and participant observation technique (Karnik and Sampath, 1977) analysed the organizational management of SITE and motivational aspects of projects like SITE. These studies have broken new grounds for the understanding of modern operational organization like television production and transmission. In the management study, one must also include the cost analysis of SITE conducted by Karnik and Sampath. In these two studies a great insight of cost analysis was presented as both these persons had worked in SITE management office and had access to first hand detailed data. Such studies are almost non-existent in the Indian context and need to be conducted in future especially in Satellite broadcasting like Indian National Satellite.

The SITE Continuity Research

In the SITE continuity phase the major thrust of research has been in the area of formative research which started in Kheda Communication Project and in other SITE Continuity areas (Mody and Rangwal 1977). After the completion of SITE some of the communication researchers who had worked on SITE social evaluation were retrained in formative research to conduct small indepth pre-production researches relating to audience profile and need assessment studies (Patel 1978a). Also script testing and pretesting of the programmes was conducted (Joshi, Trivedi and Patel, 1978). At this juncture communication researchers started working in a team mode of production of television programmes. In this mode of production, communication researchers became partners in the production process which has brought various degrees of success, much less in SITE continuity areas than in Kheda where this idea was originally propagated.

Though no large scale impact studies have been conducted in SITE continuity phase a number of small studies basicallly following the feedback methods of sample data collection have been conducted to measure the impact of individual programmes on the audience (Rajashekara Reddy and Subramanyam 1978:, Rangwala, 1980:, Singh, 1983). In this phase also great amount of care has been taken to conduct first hand studies to verify the extent to which the community televisions have been functioning properly. A major shift has been observed in the communication research from quantitative impact studies to more qualitative descriptive small studies pertaining to a particular social problem. However, none of the researchers have argued for combing both quantitative and qualitative approaches in communication research.

NOTES

1. In the morning, for extension workers and farmers, special programmes were telecast during the summer of 1976 only in Andhra Pradesh and Karnataka.

2. As almost all references of this paper have been listed in the section of Selected Bibliography, no separate reference list is attached with this paper. Readers may please refer to the bibliography section.

S R Joshi and Hansa Joshi

WOMEN AND TELEVISION : ISRO EXPERIENCES

Introduction

Kheda Communications Project (KCP) of Development and Educational Communication Unit, (DECU), Indian Space Research Organisation (ISRO) was started in 1975 along with Satellite Instructional Television Experiment (SITE). At that time a one Kilowatt transmitter was located in the Pij village of Kheda district, Gujarat State. From 1975 to 1985 Kheda TV covered about 400 villages of the district. There was a daily transmission of television programmes for one hour out of which half an hour programmes were made by India's Television authority - Doordarshan—and the remaining half hour consisting of agriculture, animal husbandry, health programmes and programmes related to social and economic issues were produced by ISRO. In July 1985 a 10 Kilo watt transmitter was established at Ahmedabad. The transmitter now covers eight districts of Gujarat State. There are estimated to be 50,000 TV sets in the coverage area consisting of 8334 villages.

There has been considerable interest, especially in recent years, about the issues of women and media. This, of course, flows from the increasing interest and action into gender equality in various fields of human activity. While accepting the definite and almost equal relationship between the broader issue of equality at large, participation of women in various spheres of activity and women - media issue, the authors in this paper are primarily examining the participation of women in India.

The paper is intended towards sharing our expeiences and approaches as far as women and television is concerned. It is hoped that it will lead to, not only pooling of experiences, but also starting a debate and raising issues.

Framework for Research

Participation of women in television can be studied from various view points. The authors have defined three broad areas for study. These are i) Participation of women as television viewers, ii) Projection of women's issues and their images on television and iii) Women as television practitioners.

This paper is based on the data from studies conducted during SITE and after SITE, at ISRO and some other studies. Some of the major sources are studies by Agrawal (1977 & 1981), Bhaskaran (1977), Joshi (1977 & 1983), Patel (1978) and Srivastava (1984).

Participation of Women as Audience

Mere intorduction of television or any other technology, does not ensure its access to the intended audience. Television access is dependent upon a variety of factors like social, cultural, economic, and political. This is especially true for the disadvantaged group. Women are definitely one such group in the Indian context. Cultural barriers, domestic duties and other taboos come in the way of women being able to view television or have access to television viewing.

Results clearly bring out that both during and after SITE, comparatively, a larger number of women of backward rural areas were unexposed to any mass media. SITE study shows 36 per cent of males and 66.5 per cent of females reported that they never listened to radio broadcast. In spite of the fact that radio was available in villages, it had not 'reached' a vast majority. Similarly, SITE survey shows that 64 per cent of rural men and 88.4 per cent of the women had never been to a cinema show. 92.8 per cent men and 95.2 per cent women had never read newspapers. 30.6 per cent men and 62.8 per cent women had never participated in any mass media before (Agrawal **et al**, 1977).

Those who got their first media exposure through SITE television were termed 'first generation mass media participants'. Among men, 20.9 per cent were first generation mass media participants, and among women this figure was 27.8 per cent. This shows that television was able to attract a higher proportion among the women than men though the number of women was smaller than those of men. (Agrawal **et al**, 1977). In another study of SITE, Bhaskaran (1977) indicated that rural women's participation in television viewing remained quite low in spite of the fact that higher portion of women were brought in the television fold during SITE. Table 1 brings out this fact clearly.

TABLE 1

Average Community Television Audiences Size per SITE Village according to Sex (Over Nine Months by States)

Sr. No.	Name of the State	Men	Women	Children	Total
1.	Andhra Pradesh	62	30	53	145
2.	Karnataka	63	20	41	124
3.	Bihar	141	57	55	253
4.	Rajasthan	54	25	46	125
5.	Orissa	76	51	39	166
6.	Madhya Pradesh	74	50	93	217
Average		78	39	55	172

Source: Bhaskaran (1977)

It may be observed from Table 1 that the average ratio of men to women participation was 2:1. It is not enough just to know the proportion of male-female viewing. It is equally important to know the reasons for not viewing television. The reasons as found in SITE studies are presented in Table 2.

TABLE 2

Reasons for not viewing Television by Sex

Reasons for Not Viewing	During SITE		After SITE	
	Male	Female	Male	Female
1. Technical limitation (of TV operation, presentation technique etc.)	12.6	9.6	10.5	11.3
2. Social restrictions (family did not allow)	1.2	12.5	2.2	13.1
3. Due to work (Domestic and agricultural)	63.5	54.2	59.2	50.2
4. Physical disability (illness etc.)	22.7	23.7	28.0	25.5

Source: Jesudasan (1977)

Table 2 indicates that it is the workload which was the

most important inhibition for both men and women from viewing television but more so for men than women. However, 'social taboo' is a much stronger restricting factor in case of females than males. Physical disability is quite an important reason in both males and females during both phases of the study. This is all the more striking when one takes into account the fact that while drawing the sample for these studies, old and infirm people were not included in the sampling frame.

Post - SITE phase results of Kheda Communication Project also indicates that the average women's participation in television viewing continued to be low. Joshi (1977) indicated that in Kheda, the average audience size was 135 (42 men, 26 women and 67 children). In other words, among of the adults viewers, 62 percent were men and 38 percent women. Patel (1978) indicated that in 1978 in Kheda the average size was 78 of which 40 percent were children and of the adults 66 percent were men and 34 percent women. According to Indian Institute of Mass Communication Study of 1982 the average audiences size in Kheda was 142 of which 48 percent were children, 33 percent were men and 15 percent women. Parmar (1983) indicated that the audience size in Kheda was 88 of which 42 percent were children and of the adults 75 percent were men and 25 percent women.

TABLE 3

Percentage Audience Composition in Kheda Communication Project between 1977-1983

	Joshi (1977)	Patel (1978)	IIMC (1982)	Parmar (1983)
Men	31	40	33	43
Women	19	20	19	15
Children	50	40	48	42
Total	100	100	100	100
Size	(135)	(78)	(142)	(88)

However, in Kheda it was observed that when women's programmes were transmitted on a regular basis at a definite time and when these programmes took into account the needs, issues, problems, and aspirations of women, the proportion of women viewers increased to about 40 percent of the adults for those programmes. It may also be noted that while participation of women increased, there was no decrease in the number of men viewers even for those programmes. This is an important point to be noted since it is important that for 'women's programmes', the men also need to be the target audience.

On the national scale a viewership study conducted by Doordarshan (1982) indicated that the total audience was 83 million out of which 23 million were women, which is about 28 percent of the total audience. But out of 83 million total audience, 33 million or 40 percent were children. Thus, while the number of women viewers is still smaller, it is not as disproportionate as found during SITE and post - SITE periods on the national scale. The main reason for this seems to be that SITE, post-Site picture pertains almost entirely to rural, community - television viewers, the Doordarshan study is mainly based on urban, individually owned television viewers - located in urban/semi-urban areas and grater accessibility. Some of the factors which hamper viewing rural community set up do not hamper in domestic situation. For example, social restrictions like women being not allowed to go out during evening hours, social customs may prevent women going to community situation,etc.

Projection of Women's Issues and Images on TV

'Women's programmes' is somewhat of a misnomer. This gives the impression that the programmes are meant for women alone, and that the target audience is women alone. This kind of situation may have value in certain contexts but the authors believe that for many of the women's programmes, men should **also** be the target audience. Women's programmes, therefore, should have a broader definition to include all programmes dealing with the issues, problems and aspirations of women. This definition of women's programmes has the advantage of making them much more broad based and can bring in women's dimension in all aspects of programming and not confining it to stereotype of cookery and child care.

One of the things to look at is how much time is given to 'special audience programmes' or women's programmes. In April 1983, there were about 1.6 percent of women's programmes, if taken into account all the production centres of Doordarshan (Srivastava, 1984). Considering the fact that 48 percent are the adult female viewers the figure of 1.6 percent is indeed very low.

Classification of SITE programmes did not have a category called "women's programmes" and no data are available about women's programmes. After SITE, Kheda programmes of ISRO have had a category of women's programmes. Table 4 indicates the percentage of time for women's programmes produced by ISRO.

TABLE 4

Yearwise percentages of Women's Programmes

Year	Percentage of Women's Programmes
1978	6
1979	5
1980	3
1981	7
1982	3
1984	5
1985	11

Source: Yearly Transmission Analysis, ISRO.

As stated earlier the percentage of women's programmes is only one criterion to look at. What one should also examine is the issues and problems taken up in women's programmes. Do they present stereotypes of women as housewife, mother etc. or her newer roles are brought out? Are the subjects still stereotyped like embroidery, cookery, child care etc. or do they embark upon larger issues pertaining to women? Even more important is whether attention is paid, from this angle, to only 'women's programmes' or are all other programmes looked at having women's domension whether it is agriculture or sports or socioeconomic issues or even entertainment programmes.

The authors would like to examine women's programmes from this perspective. It is also in this context that formative research will have a crucial role to play. The researchers should be able to provide inputs from this perspective so that the real issues and problems are brought out, the programmes become need based, it must not reinforce traditional beliefs and images or stereotypes. The women's dimension is brought out in its totality and not confined to women's programmes alone.

As far as protrayal of women is concerned, there have been large number of articles especially by women's groups. But the authors are not aware of any systematic content analysis study of Doordarshan programmes from this perspective.

Research in Women's Programme Production

In ISRO almost all our women's programmes have been made as a collaborative effort between the producer and the researcher. Detailed field studies have been conducted to find out the conditions, the problems and needs of women as well as the situations affecting women. Both quantitative as well as qualitative methodologies have been adopted depending upon the need of situation.

A field study in Kheda villages indicated that not only is the women's status low but also that the women lacked in self-confidence and very often had a very low self-image of themselves. There was good deal of internalisation of feeling inferiority amongst the women and discrimination was accepted as the given thing. A major reason for this was that the women were economically dependant upon others. If the status of the woman was to be improved and she was to be made more self-confident, it was necessary to start a series aimed at increasing her economic independence. It was from this view point that a series called 'Nari - Tún - Nárayani' (Women You are Strength) was started to promote cooperative, economic activities.

Due to lack of research on the problems of rural women, background research had to be done. Needs assessment studies had to be conducted to find out the basic needs to which a programme or a series of programmes should be addressed. Determination of entry skills, needs assessment studies and background research became prerequisite to mounting of a series which had well defined objective and which can become an effective communication tool. When we took up a series on women and law called 'Nyay - Anyay' (Justice-Injustice) we found that merely knowing the technical information about the law was not enough. We also had to determine the level of knowledge of both men and women, the difficulties they experience while making use of the law and the social or economic factors which prevent its effective use. We also found that this information had to be presented in such a manner which can be easily comprehended by a common villager.

Programme Pretesting

Pretesting was aimed at determining the attention holding ability of the programme, its comprehension, effectiveness of the format, personal relevance, identification, believability and acceptability. When we pretested 'Nyay - Anyay' (Justice - Industice) programme, we found that the play format part was less attention and comprehension. It was therefore decided that the discussion with the lawyers had to be made in a very simple and common person's language and that it should not be too long. Repetition of the major points was also considered to be necessary for better comprehension. When this was done it was found that the programmes became more effective.

Brief Writing

Detailed brief writings have been found to be effective. The brief includes information on the target audience, the objective, the content and the major question which needs to be tested. It is found that when the programme is based on such brief it is much better goal directed.

Feedback Evaluation

We conducted feedback studies very often. The feedback provided information on attention holding ability, likes and dislikes, comprehension, identification, personal relevance and whether there was anything offending in the programme.

Impact Evaluation

We have conducted some small summative evaluative studies on the women's programmes and it was found that the programmes had taken up issues which were relevant to women. They had helped them in doing or starting something new or had indicated different ways of thinking and analysing an issue. Some of the findings of these research studies are summarized here.

Results of Feeback and Summative Evaluations

All viewers, especially the women, like to see play formats most. A continuous story line attracts more, than programmes of single episode. However, if a programme is based on a true incident, the audience prefers to see the concerned real people narrating their own experiences, stories etc. and this is considered to have greater impact on them for example the programme **Bhadke Bale Chhe Jindagi** (Life is in Flames).

- Most women want that programmes should take up 'real' incidents/ situations or issues relevant to them, but want to see a positive end, even if it is 'unreal'. It is felt that while being conscious of reality is important, it is equally important that the end should be such that new directions or solutions are suggested.

The most suitable time for women is found to be between 8 to 9 p.m. because it is only after 8 p.m. that women finish the household chores and get time to watch television.

- Women's programmes should not be addressed to women alone, but both women an men should the target audience.

Women as Media Practitioners

These days, considerable attention is paid to the question of portrayal of women on television and the question of access to television. It is true that even in this area not many systematic studies are available. But there is an increased awareness and a large number of articles, small studies and focus of many debates and discussions at various fora. However, the problem of women media practitioners - the source - has been studied to a very small extent. We have recently conducted the first study about women practitioners in television (Doordarshan) at creative and decision making levels. The main findings of this study are presented here. In this study primary and secondary data were utilized.

There were three main sources of information.

(1) Statistical data were gathered from the existing information of employment in Doordarshan.

(2) The second source of information was personal interviews at different levels.

(3) The third source of information was a mailed questionnaire.

The major findings of the study were:

- Percentage of women producers is about 26 percent in Doordarshan. It may be noted that in European Economic Community countires this figures is also about the same.

- Apart from producers there are very few women employees at higher decision making levels e.g. station directors, engineers, administrative officers.

- Available statistics do not support the widely held belief among men that the proportion of women in Doordarshan is rapdily increasing.

- Discrimination in Doordarshan organization was not considered to be an important reason for lesser proportion of women.

- Social and domestic responsibilities of women were considered to be most important barriers e.g. child care, cooking, etc.

- There was no difference in the work satisfaction of women and men.

- Larger number of men considered women to be incapable of independent, quick decision making.

- Larger number of women considered women officers to be less considerate than men officers.

- A much greater number of men thought that they are exploited by women and that women took advantage of men's chivalry.

- A much larger number of women thought that by increasing the proportion of women the programme quality will improve and they would bring a more balanced perspective.

- More men considered that their work increased while working with colleagues belonging to the opposite sex.

- Lack of availability of trained women was considered to be a very important reason for lower proportion of women.

- much larger number of women felt that there is less proportion of women because the selection committees consisted mostly of men.

- There were strong job stereotypes and women were considered unsuitable for many jobs. Women employees thought that they were typecast by the organization.

In Conclusion

We have examined our work and some other studies pertaining to women and television in India. It is hoped that some of these findings will be of interest to other researchers. Even more important would be if more research studies are taken up in this area. We have put together only a small area of research but many more detailed research studies need to be conducted. Some of the important questions that come to mind on which research needs to be conducted are: How women can have greater access to television? How to make them participate in programmes of their concern? How many programmes should there be for women? What type of programme are needed for women? Is women's dimension properly taken up in general programmes? Does the overall juxtaposition of programmes wipe out the effects of some good programmes? How to increase participation of women media practitioners? and, How to share experience between researchers?

We are sure that there will be many more questions into which research needs to be conducted.

REFERENCES

1. Agrawal, B.C. : SITE Social Evaluations: Results, Experiences and Implications, Space Applications Centre, Indian Space Research Organisation, 1981, Ahmedabad.

2. Agrawal, B.C., J.K. Doshi, Victor Jesudasan, K.K. Verma: Satellite Instructional Television Experiment Social Evaluation - Impact on Adults,SAC,ISRO, September, 1977, Ahmedabad.

3. Bhaskaran, P.: SITE Evening Feedback Report, 1977, SAC, ISRO.

4. Directorate General, Doordarshan : TV Audience Survey, December, 1981, New Delhi.

5. Gallagher, Margaret : Employment and Positive Action for Women in the Television Organization of the EEC Member States, 1984, London.

6. Indian Institute of Mass Communcation:, An Assessment of Community Viewing and Listening Schemes, 1982, New Delhi.

7. Joshi, S.R. : 'The Invisible Barriers', Development and Educational Communication Unit, Indian Space Research Organization, January, 1986, Ahmedabad.

8. Joshi, S.R. : Gatekeepers at Receiving End, SAC, ISRO, September, 1983, Ahmedabad.

9. Joshi, Subhash : Kheda TV Operation Study, SAC, ISRO, 1977 Ahmedabad.

10. Joshi, Hansa : 'Nari Tun Narayani', Sanshodhanno Drashtikon, SAC, ISRO, January, 1984.

11. Joshi, Hansa, 'Bhadke Bole Chhe Jindgi', SAC, ISRO, October, 1985.

12. Kalwachwala, Dinaz and Hansa Joshi - "Experiences of Women's Programme, Producer - Researcher Interaction" 1984.

13. KCP Researchers : Monthly Transmission Analysis of ISRO Programmes, DECU, ISRO, Ahmedabad.

14. Patel, Ila : Kheda TV Operation Study, SAC, ISRO, 1978, Ahmedabad.

15. Parmer, K.M. : Kheda Audience Composition Study, SAC, ISRO, Ahmedabad, 1983.

16. Srivastava, U.K. : The Cost of Doordarshan Programmes for Women and Children : Some Preliminary Estimates, working paper No.526, Indian Insitute of Management, Ahmedabad.

Binod C Agrawal

RELEVANCE OF HOLISTIC APPROACH IN COMMUNICATION RESEARCH : THE INDIAN EXPERIENCE

The paper that the author attempts to present on the holistic approach in communication research has been recently documented in an edited book (Agrawal, 1985). The aim is to bring out some of the salient points along with a strong plea to emphasize the utility of holistic approach in communication research in South Asia and in other Third World countires. Holistic approach in communication research is not even 10 years old. Of course, a number of references have been made and scholars adhering to quantitative large scale survey methods, have begun to question the usefulness of quantitative methods as the only best means for the understanding of effects of television communiation and process of television communication. It is in this spirit that some who came to television research from other disciplines like anthropology, began to doubt the real utility of quantitative methods as the only means of understanding television effects. Also, some have repeatedly questioned the validity of a universal method for understanding social processes and social realities.

The formative researchers have emphasised tirelessly that the steps and procedures that have to be followed in the production of a television programme is almost applicable to any country and culture. I wonder whether this assertion would even be test worthy. Without getting into the argument, I would like to share my experiences with holistic approach for communication research in the real life situation in a multilinguistic, multi-religious and historically old civilization like India. The possible use of non-survey methodology for understanding both communication process and effects has shown a new path - both for theory building and planning purposes.

Historical Development

Recently the effect of this development in communication research has given an interesting positive feedback to anthropologists in India, who have started incorporating

"Communication Anthropology" as a new field to be taught as a part of the syllabus for graduate students. The holistic method in anthropology is as old as the discipline itself. Therefore, it is not very difficult, for the anthropologist to adapt holistic method in researches, focusing on communication except that they have started familiarising themselves with the issues related to communication and communication theory. This two way flow of information, in my opinion, is going to enrich the communication discipline and also enlarge the field of investigation for anthropologists. This is not an isolated instance in India but, there are indications that in several schools of communication there is a growing intereest in holistic approach to communication research. For example, East-West Communication and Culture Institute in the United States of America, Centre for Mass Communication Research in United Kingdom and several such institutions have started encouraging students to follow the holistic approach.

My own involvement in communication research began with Satellite Instructional Television Experiment (SITE) 1973. At that time a need was felt by the experimenters "Who were basically urban trained, knowledgeable scientists, engineers, managers, and producers to know their audience". Today, I am not sure how much these audience profiles prepared were actually used or were appropriate for producers. But certainly, it laid the foundation of a new tradition of both research and television production methods.

Holistic Approach

Let me just briefly describe what the holistic approach involves as a method as well as a philosophy in understanding human culture and behaviour, vis-a-vis human and electronic communication. Generally, anthropologists as compared to other social scientists wish to understand all the manifestations of human beings and their activities, in a unified perspective conceiving of all these manifestations and activities as a whole. They resist any simplistic and reductionist explanation of socio-cultural phenomena: communication being one such phenomenon. Basically, anthropologists throw their net of investigation in the largest arena of human-biological as well as socio-cultural, implicit and explicit, widely connected and unconnected factors that might help explain human hehaviour. Even psychological, economic, political, and ecological dimensions are touched upon carefully, to understand human beings and their activities. This in a way assumes inter-linkages and inter-connectedness of almost all socio-cultural behaviour that could be understood and explained by carefully analysing each of its mainfestations in a systematic manner.

Another area, which anthropologists have been emphasising relates to the understanding of process. And if communication is an act and a process, then it must be studied as a cultural act, as well as a process. In this perspective, if one has a holistic approach of human hehaviour then the dynamic process that helps evolve newer forms of relationships and behaviour as a result of continual interaction and activity must be analysed as a process. "Applications of such a perspective would help analyse communication acts as a process in different social situations and role relationships" (Agrawal, 1985:19).

Another critical issue in social science research is the use of categories or systematizing or organising any set of data. In anthropology the "**emic approach**" has gained greater acceptance as it permits the use of culturally defined categories and classification for data systematization and interpretation. In the case of India, it has relevance, both at the analytical level, and understanding level. Quite often, a simple categorization of social class builds a barrier instead of facilitating a communication behaviour. For example, sociological literature in order to provide meaningful social categories has devised concepts like upper, middle, and lower social classes. The division is based on statistical and economic distribution of a national population of many American and European countries. It is also based on several social attributes of a given society. Having a larger acceptability of such class categories, applied in the Indian situation, provides disastrous results when more than three-fourths of the population falls either below the poverty line or just above it. To me this is a very unjustified and unrealistic classification, as it provides a skewed distribution. In a situation like this, **emic** category would probably help understand the class distribution in a more realistic manner. Terms like **Dhani** (rich) and **Garib** (poor) as class categories manifest, both social and economic characterisitic of the class. It is because of this reason that the emic approach for the understanding of communication behaviour will minimize spurious analyses and interpretations in India and other Third World countries.

Let me give another example which creates research problems in rural communication studies in India and elsewhere. The word "village" in English language in no way reflects the concept of an agrarian settlement in differnt lingustic regions of India. Historically the English language when uniformally imposed by the colonial rulers, approximated a concept of village with defined area from where agricultural revenue could be collected from the land. This led to the development of the concept of the revenue village in India and in many British colonies. Social scientists today, go at length to debate the concept of village in English language without giving due consideration to the fact that what is universally accepted as village in English language, is not really an Indian village of a given lingustic region. A great deal of emic research for understanding agrarian human settlements is needed before village as a special category could be used for analysis. In order to evolve any universal social categories for general explanation or for building a general theory of any kind it would be most important to develop a comparative perspective which anthropologists believe is essential, especially, if one is interested in the comparison of communication processes. An understanding of the communication process in most cases requires continuous observation of the community or group under study. This can only be done through participant observation. Participant observation..." involves participating in the day-to-day life of the people being studied by living with them over an extended period of time" (Olien 1978:19).

Since SITE, I have been advocating the holistic approach in communication research and it has been fairly well accepted not only in India, but outside India in other Third World countries. As a matter of fact, several communication researchers from Eurpoe and America have pointed out that if one wishes to have a little "flesh and meat" in the findings one ought to collect descriptive in-depth data, in addition to dry statistics. I endorese this view based on our experience during SITE . It would not be out of place to mention that, encouraged from our past experience we plan to conduct a "re-visit" study of nine SITE villages after 10 years.

We aim to not only study social change, but also changes in communication behaviour, and the effects of communication as an agent of change in the rural culture. In this study, once again, a period of 3-6 months will be spent in the field for participant observation. Original field notes, collected in 1975-76, will be compared with the present data especially in the areas of media acquisition, and media utilization, and the remnants, if any, from the television exposure in 1975-76.

Methodological Strategy

The methodological startegy that emerges from the holistic approach in communiation research is based on the assumption that like other social processes, communication is an activity for transmission of information and process for maintaining human relations. It also assumes that there is an explicit cultural ethos that regulates communication behaviour in all aspects of human life and in its actual operation it gets modified either through its own hidden energy or the stimulant of externally generated energy. This communication transcends linguistic competence and interlocks several other social activities for smooth exchange and transaction of day-do-day activities. The decoding of the messages is only possible by those belonging to the same cultural milieu. It remains ambiguous to provide varying interpretations and meanings to generate confusion, tension, and misinformation. It is these factors that lead to hidden energy of communication to create dynamism in the communication process. Values and ideologies though used interchangeably depending upon the perspective of the social scientist remain at the core of communication activity and process. I think that if you accept this holistic methodological strategy you will be able to bridge quite a bit of gap between the different theoretical stands on the role of communication in development and its relationships with the social and political structure in which it operates. To some extent, communication then as an activity and process assumes a super-organic and autonomous position in the hierarchy of social institutions that determines the direction and dynamism of cultural forces. More than fifty years ago an American anthropologist claimed that culture is superorganic (Kroeber 1917).I personally think that the communication element of culture is certainly superorganic and needs to be understood within this framework.

All I am arguing here is that there is a great need for using holistic approach in communication research which is still a fast growing discipline of diverse interests and views. Holistic approach will provide an integrated methodology to cater to the needs of diverse views and ideas.

REFERENCES

Agrawal, Binod C. (ed) (1985) Anthropological Methods for Communication Research.New Delhi: Concept Publishing Company.

Kroeber, A (1917) The Superorganic. **American Anthropologist,** Vol. 19:163-213.

Olien, Michael, D. (1978) The Human Myth : An Indroduction of Anthropology. New York : Harper and Row Publishers.

Arbind Sinha

PROBLEMS OF FIELD DATA COLLECTION IN COMMUNICATION RESEARCH

Field work or data collection is a very important aspect of any research, specially in social sciences including communication. In the field of communication, research is mostly confined to media research, particularly media effects studies. Indian Space Research Organisation (ISRO) have been involved in conducting two types of communication researches. These are: quick and dirty research and indepth research. Both have their own value and relevance. The first is a quick reflection of what happens immediately after the viewers are exposed to the communication and the second gives a full understanding of the whole communication process. A few social scientists, mainly anthropologists, have touched the cultural aspects of communication also.

The history of ISRO's involvement in communication research goes back to 1973 when a couple of social scientists and communication researchers were invited to conduct social impact studies of Satellite Instructional Television Experiment (SITE) wherein 2330 villages of six states of India were exposed to television for a year between August 1975 to July 1976. After completion of SITE a small but permanent 'Social Study Group' was set up within ISRO to carry on different social sciences related studies including communication research. Although ISRO works with sophisticated technology like applications of satellite, the focus of communication research has been the rural areas, may it be direct broadcast through satellite, disaster warning system, remote sensing, or video revolution. Occasional urban studies have also been undertaken with greater emphasis on first hand field study. Social scientists in ISRO have been conducting quantitative as well as qualitative studies. In this paper the attempt will be made to document the experiences in the field of communication research. First let me describe two levels of field experiences of the social scientists.

A 'research manager' flies down to the State capital where a vehicle is waiting to receive the research manager. The vehicle takes him to a metting where he collects a lot of information from State officials. The data have been collected. When he reaches to the office his colleagues ask - "How was the trip"? The answer generally is - "Oh fine, I happened to visit the field, I collected the data myself".

There is another situation where a field researcher gets down from a local train and continues the field journey by an over crowded bus. Upon arrival at the bus-stop he is told that he has to walk for several kilometers to reach the village he wants to visit. This journey starts on the hilly tracks of a tribal area but the researcher feels much comfortable than in the bus. When he reaches to the village he finds no place to stay. On the mercy of a few good villagers the researcher might be accommodated in a village hut. Anyway, he collects the required data and somehow comes back from the field trip. Everybody mechanically ask - "How did you enjoy your field" Yes, he enjoyed it. It was an experience and in the Indian situation there is no end to this type of experience.

The above two descriptions of the field work conducted by two levels of researchers in two different contexts and in two different modes raise basic questions about organisational structurel, the heirarchy in data collection and hence the validity of the data. For sure, the primary data is collected by the latter type of researchers and it is his/her experiences that I would like to share.

Problems of Data Collection

Before we discuss the problems of field data collection, it is desirable to understand the process and organisational structure of data collection in the Indian context. Data collection is done either by "full time" or "part-time","daily wages", or project staff. In the field of communication, majority of the data are collected by project staff of one kind or the other. Research design and planning is the responsibility of the senior "Research Managers" and "Project Directors". They take all major decisions about the sampling, data collection procedure, analysis and report writing. The field staff are, in many cases, responsible for data collection, coding and table preparation. The emphasis here is on the experiences of data collected by the field staff. The focus will be rural India where ISRO has conducted several national level studies. The field data collection experiences, both of descriptive and survey types, are presented in two categories (a) rural literates, and (b) rural illiterates. Some efforts will also be made to discuss about the problems related to the selection of respondents in the field situation and nature of data collected, especially on economic aspects.

The Rural Literates

The percentage of literacy in rural India does not exceed 30 per cent and those who can understand the social research and the researchers are few.

The researcher when in the rural millieu wants to meet those literates who would understand his questions and problems and can respond to him. Obviously, the choice is narrowed down to a few individuals. In most of the cases, they belong to the upper castes/upper income group, and are well exposed to the outside would (in the local context the block or taluka office or nearby cities). They have good connections with the **Panchayat** (village council) and block administrative officials and other development agencies. They are either employed or managing agricultural farm or unemployed youth loitering in the village. It is not only our experience but that of many other researchers that this group is the most cooperative in providing data. Particularly the third category is invariably ready to welcome any visitor, including researcher, from outside. They have time to entertain and help the researcher. They accompany the researcher and help in establishing contact with other respondents. Sometimes the schedules are also filled up by these 'friends'. When I was doing my SITE field work and had to go out of the village, one such friend used to maintain attendance register of the TV viewers for me. They are also, in many cases, the key informants.

The reasons why they are so cooperative are many. One reason is that the literates do not hesitate in talking to another person whom they consider educated. They want to have more information from outside and take the researcher to be more knowledgeable and well informed. They also feel that their being in good contact of the researcher adds to their prestige in the village. For the unemployed youth, researcher's company is a good time passing activity. The old people also feel glad that instead of loitering here and there these young people are spending their time with an educated person who may be benefical to them, atleast in guiding for better future.

The scene changes in the anthropological field work particularly when the researcher stays in a village for a fairly long time. In this situation, there are a few literates, belong to highest income group who control the power politics of the village do not feel comfortable. Sometimes their status and superiority complex in them also comes in the way. They are the first who want to patronise the researcher and do not like the researcher to interact with others. Failing this they try to keep a distance. When the villagers start consulting the researcher for suggestion these educated "power elites" who are also often the opinion leaders, feel threatened. One good way of handling this situation would be to maintain distance and cordial relation with every one and to be very careful towards these "power elites".

Rural Illiterates

The rural illiterates are obedient to the extent that many of the researchers keep them engaged for hours because they do not object to it. We write papers, thesis, report or stories and they do not know of it. But it does not mean that they do everything gladly or cooperatively because they want to cooperate. No, it is mainly because in rural India a visitor is welcome and to help a visitor is considered a great service to the humanity and the God. This is one reason that conducting field studies in rural India is considered easier than in urban India.

The rural illiterates though welcoming, are totally unaware of the motives of the study. Hence, often different interpretations are given by different individuals leading to a suspecion about the researcher who goes on asking odd questions. Of course, a prolonged visit helps a lot but the initial rapport building is a task which should be handled carefully by the researchers.

The informant's ignorance about many issues creats problem and repeated probing is required. Cross checking of data is suggested not because the respondents do not want to provide correct information but what comes immediately in their mind they tell to the researcher which may not be the correct one. As mentioned in the proceeding pages, initially, the identity of the researcher is questioned. At this stage, the data given to the researcher is subject to cross checking. It is the personal experience of the author that at the initial stages, the data quality was different than what he got after staying in the village for some time. When asked why there was difference between the two sets of data, the villagers innocently said that "during the first few meetings you were not a part of our village family. Now, even if we say anything incorrect, you are here to check the authenticity".

Selection of Respondents

Selection of respondents remain an important methodological

issue in communication research, Both quantitative as well as qualitative researches depend heavily on the right type of respondents otherwise the quality of the data remains weak. Qualitative methods give a little flexibility and the researcher follows a broad "interview guide" or "field guide" and selects the respondents, depending upon the field situation. But survey method has to follow a rigid sampling method and these samples are drawn keeping statistical parameters in mind. In most of the cases it does not take into account the field realities. Very often when the researcher finds that drawing of proper sampling is not possible he/she gets puzzled. No need to mention that respondents in the field, in both rural and urban settings, are concerned about their own convenience and not necessary readily available.

Any random sample in rural India will have a large proportion of landless illiterate labour as respondents. On reaching the village you find that most of the labourers have migrated, temporarily, to the nearby construction site and only a small per cent of the selected sample is available in the field. In this situation one needs an alternate planning and margin of time to adjust changes in the sample. The field researcher should be in a position to decide about the substitute. As already mentioned, often field studies are conducted by daily wage field researchers who do not have proper understanding about the research design or do not have enough understanding of delicacies of research. They find it difficult to take an alternate decision. It is also true that due to lack of understanding of the research design they take steps which are not desirable. Recently, for a survey a researcher in the field was requested to take a sample of 60 students ; 30 from an experimental group and 30 from a control group from the same class in the same school. The field researcher found that all the students of that particular class have been exposed to the experiment so the researcher was in a difficult position. Immediately 30 experimental students were taken from one school and 30 control students were taken from another experimental school. It is a useless data. This was because of communication as well as understanding gap. Proper training also comes in the way. It is a general experience that whatever research methodology we are taught in the class room provides only a limited understanding. The real methods of research are developed while working in the field situation. This adds to the experience to be utilised for the next field work.

Getting Data on Economic Aspects

Socio-economic data is one of the very important component of most of the social as well as communication research. But getting data on the economic aspect of the individual, household, or the community is a most difficult task and the experiences say that whatever data researchers get is just a base to arrive at some approximation. In urban situation, the respondents, except a few salaried persons who disclose their income indicated on the "salary slip", do not have any idea of income or they do not want or like to disclose the real income. Even among the educated and salaried respondents if the question is asked about the budget heads for the household expenditure chances are very high that a very rough estimate would be provided. The first question the respondent would ask- "Why do you want to know all these things?" For big businessmen even giving a rough estimate will pose certain doubts and they question the confidentiality of the data. It is a hard task for the researcher to convince the respondents to give a correct picture of income. Of course, the labourers do not have anything to hide.

In the rural areas, no systematic record is kept for income and expenditure. Even the rough estimate will be known only to the head of the household who may not be in a mood to oblige the researcher. Very often an answer like - "Whatever is left after meeting all the household and other expenditures is our income" irritates the researcher but that is the way the villagers calculate income and expenditure. Getting an estimate of income is not an easy task. A typical answer to an income question will be "the total product this year was 50 quintals of paddy, 10 quintals of wheat, 3 quintals of chillies, 2 truck loads of sugar cane, and one quintal of oil seed". Now it is up to the researcher to calculate the estimated cost of all these products. Needless to say that the cost of these agricultural products depends highly on the quality of the product as well as the season when it is to be sold in the market. Do the researcher has time and proper information to calculate the accurate income?

The easiest method used by most of the researchers collecting economic data is to find out the total land holding of the individual or household and calculate on the basis of average yield per acre and average cost of the produce. But getting an idea of the land holding itself is a herculian task. Let us look at the possible sources of such data. Revenue land record is available with the Village Level Worker or the revenue record man at the village level. One is really lucky if he can get hold of these functionaries and get something out of them. This record indicates the land owned by an individual or household. The total land owned may not necessarily fall within the geographical boundaries of the village. It does not tell if informant X owns land in village Y for which no record is maintained by this record keeper. Other problem is that a plot of land is recorded on the name of X who died long ago and the property is inherited by five households living in three different villages. Looking into the realities of village India the ownership pattern is such that 10-15 per cent of the household owns 70-75 per cent of the land and invariably the ownership crosses the geographical boundaries of the village. This problem can be tackled if the researcher has enough time and he/she is not visiting a village for a day or two for the purposes of data collection.

Life in the Village

The field investigator while staying in the field, particularly when the stay is longer, is expected to maintain a modest life. The purpose is to minimise the gap between the general living condition of the villagers and that of the researcher. But in practice, it is a hard task. The biggest problem in this state of art is that the researcher as a student learns to live cleanly. Though the researchers in many cases try to adopt the life style of the field but to keep everything in order makes him little different than the rest. Raju (1985:54) writes, "In order to present an image of myself as a member of the village community, I adorned the village costume, a **lungi** and a shirt and in my visit to the school, I wore trousers, for the school teacher have trousers. This distinction in dress was clearly marked in the village, highlighting the significance of the educated individual". Rai (1985:112) informs, "I fell sick and hence returned to my home in Lucknow. In my absence, the village women helped my husband in household chores. They cooked his meals and cleaned and swept the rooms."

Pandey (1985:119) describing his first week of fieldwork in Rajasthan village writes, "The week however was torturous, for the food offered to me consisting of thick barleygram - wheat, mixed bread, curry made of green flour, turmeric powder, ghee and chilly was hot and spicy. I could not eat more than a morsel. It was a week of starvation and I survived on the few packets of biscuits that I had brought from Jaipur". I was also marked by villagers of Ismailpur (Bihar) during my study because of my pressure cooker, kerosine stove, and for hiring a made survant to clean the utensiles (Sinha 1985).

Self Identification of Identity

Identification of the researcher is also a methodological question for any kind of field research in rural India. During Satellite Instructional Television Experiment (SITE) study an uniform training at Space Applications Centre, Ahmedabad helped us a lot in identifying ourselves. We repetatively said "we want to study the impact of TV on the village life and we belong to Research and Evaluation Cell of Space Applications Centre, Ahmedabad". We were identified atleast, initially, by the respective groups of villagers differently at different times. Raju (1985:54) wrote, "Trying to build a rapport with villagers was not easy. Initially, some of the villagers suspected me to be a spy or CID (a person from Central Intelligence Department). Their suspicion was affirmed when a project leader visited (me) after a few weeks of my stay. He had, during this occasion, parked his jeep ahead of the village before entering and carried a camera with him while walking through the streets of the village. Similarly, two young Madiga youth thought that I was a government official, campaigning for family planning."

Jha (1985:67) observed that "The educated adults, associated with the CPI (Communist Party of India) took me to be CIA (Central Intelligence Agency) agent. The CPI leader Thakur spoke to me atleast ten times a week and watched my movements closely.... The other Communist leaders also considered me to be a propagandist of the Congress Government.... The lower jatis such as Chamer, Paswan, Mallah and Dhanuk perceived me as a person in-charge of distributing ration cards". Sinha (1985) reports "In my initial acquaintance, I met with some hostility from the villagers for a rumour had spread that I was from the CBI (Central Bureau of Investigation). Still others treated me as a doctor sahib, for the village doctor had previously resided in the room I stayed in. The community hall was meant for VLW so some of them thought that I was a Village Level Worker. In short, I was a stranger and the villagers were not clear about my purpose of visit". Ravi P. Rai and Kumkum Rai who studied the village Kedli of Rajasthan caused anxieties in the mind of their landlord for his brother suspected them to be a government employee, reporting about the corruption in the village, (Rai 1985:97-105). Describing his experiences Pandey (1985:199-120) writes, "In the beginning the villagers were sceptical about my role. When I went to meet a farmer in his farm, he would neither shut off the pump or leave the farm. He would refused to speak to me. This was due to their suspicion and fear that I was a government official. Government officials from the Revenue, Electricity and Police Department often harassed the villagers and fleeded them either directly or when afforded by an opportunity."

Writing Field Notes/Daily Diaries

For any indepth study the field diary of the researcher is

the basic document which contains all the data collected by him/her and hence careful/confidential preservation of the diary is essential. It is a general practice to write two kinds of field notes; (a) Brief note on the spot, and (b) a detailed daily diary. The detailed daily field diary also contains details of observation and personal interpretation. In practice, both the formulae fails miserably. In rural situation the moment the researcher starts writing anything or taking notes of anything, informants become suspicious about it. They will gather around the researcher and try to read the notes. Everybody starts looking at the researcher and disturbes the situation. On occasions like funeral it is almost unhuman that some one writes anything. Marriages take place, in places like rural Bihar and Eastern Uttar Pradesh, in the night and there would be no proper lighting arrangements that a researcher could write anything. In this circumstances, a symbolic note in code words helps a lot and researcher writes the field diary from it. For writing a detailed field diary, concentration is required so that the researcher could think properly, recall the moments he had spent with the people and write it in a sequence. But it is a common experience that at many occasions, it is found very difficult to get free time for it. Needless to mention that any delay in writing the field diary amounts to loss of data as well as increasing burden for writing on part of the researcher. It is my personal experience that very often the villagers would sit in researcher's room gossiping and chewing tobacco. They leave the room late in the night and the writing of the field diary can start only after that. This writing of daily diary late in the night put many of the villagers into doubt. Similar type of problem has been experienced by Rai (1985:103). He writes, "...I encountered some constraints which were detrimental to the daily schedule. One such constraint was the arrival of guests at late hours of the night. The villagers would get together at my home. In their enthusiasm to learn more about me and discuss and talk about many issues, they would sit many hours, at times even till early morning, which upset my routine for the day". Rai was a married man and was living in the village with his family. The same happened with me when my wife stayed in the village for a short period during my field work in Ismailpur (Bihar). Against the will of my wife I had to entertain the villagers who will come any time late in the evening and would continue sitting till late in the night.

It is suggested to write the field notes and diaries in local language. But it creates a dialemma to the researcher. As mentioned earlier, villagers, if finds the researchers writing something, have a tendency to try to read as to what the researcher is writing. May be they have a fear that something is written against them. If the note is in the language easy for them to understand the researcher will have difficult time in keeping the confidentiality of the data. And if it is written in code words or a language not comprehensive to the village creats a suspicion in their mind. I had a bitter experience while conducting my field work in Varanasi (Uttar Pradesh). The religious priests saw me taking notes of the rituals being performed. In spite of the fact that they all knew that I was doing field work for a research project they became suspicious. One of them came closer and tried to read it. When he could not read anything out of it he just snatched away the note book and others tried to read it. The matter was taken to the head priest who knew me well. I had hard time in interpreting the notes and convincing the priests about its harmlessness.

Apart from all these problems the biggest problem in collecting data from the field has been government rules to reimburse the travel and living cost which governs most of the projects run and financed by the government. Unless one is ready to loose money from his/her pocket the fast and smooth data collection is difficult and the fact remains that one who is employed on salary would not like to loose money from the pocket. As a result of this, the quality of data collection suffers. Unfortunately, those who can modify the rules are not affected hence they do not realise the probelm.

REFERENCES

Ambedkar, J.B. (1985) The Good Officials. In Anthropological Methods for Communication Research, Binod C. Agrawal (ed) pp. 87–93. New Delhi: Concept Publishing Company.

Jha, M.N. (1985) A village by the Kosi River. In Anthropological Methods for Communication Research, Binod C. Agrawal (ed) pp. 63–69. New Delhi: Concept Publishing Comapny.

Pandey, K.K. (1985) The 'Ghost' village. In Anthropological Methods for Communication Research, Binod C. Agrawal (ed) pp. 117–121. New Delhi: Concept Publishing Company.

Rai, Ravi P. (1985) A Lie can be Half-Truth. In Anthropological Methods for Communication Research, Binod C. Agrawal (ed) pp. 97–105. New Delhi: Concept Publishing Company.

Rai, Kumkum (1985) Behind the Veil. In Anthropological Methods for Communication Research, Binod C. Agrawal (ed) pp. 109–114. New Delhi: Concept Publishing Comapny.

Raju, M.V.T. (1985) The Old Nizam Village. In Anthropological Methods for Communication Research, Binod C. Agrawal (ed) pp. 51–59. New Delhi: Concept Publishing Company.

Sinha, Arbind K. (1985a) The Moments in Quietness. In Anthropological Methods of Communication Research, Binod

C. Agrawal (ed) pp. 73-84. New Delhi: Concept Publishing Company.
Sinha, Arbind K. (1985b) Role of Mass Media in Rural Development. New Dlehi: Concept Publishing Company.

Bela Trivedi

COMMUNICATION SUPPORT FOR YOUTH EMPLOYMENT

Working in the field of development communication has been a continuous learning process, it has shattered my many myths, removed many misconceptions. As a formative researcher for Kheda Communication Project[1] I have been constantly interacting with the television viewers to study their knowledge, attitude, and communication needs.

Research studies of Kheda TV viewers indicated the need to focus on youth[2] Initially it was thought to highlight the problem, difficulties, aspirations and feelings of the youth on television screen. Among the needs "employment needs" topped the list. The idea was discussed with other colleagues who not only appreciated but encouraged to the extent that this research became a mission.

The idea of employment programmes struck while going through a paper received from Branch Recruiting Officer of Army for publicity for recruitment to Armed Forces at Dakor, Kheda on 18th June, 1980. Since Army regularly conducts such camps, a proposal was made to support this effort by using TV as a medium of information. Accordingly, we outlined the objectives as to: (a) impart information about Army recruitment and recruitment camps, (b) provide information about educational and physical requirements, (c) emphasise on economic gains, (d) remove fear about Armed Forces and (e) warn people against unauthorised self-appointed agents of employment.

Approach

After assessing the youth knowledge and attitudes towards Armed Forces, pre-recruitment motivational and informative programmes were produced. Keeping their immediate needs in view, the appeal was on economic and rational grounds. Announcements informing the day, date, recruitment place and required educational qualifications. Television programmes were transmitted a week prior to the recruitment date. These included three minutes announcements and a documentary of 18 minutes. In addition, two motivational plays were produced to support the effort.

Responce

An attempt was made to obtain feedback during the camp and had personal discussions with the prospective candidates who had responded positively. For the first time, heavy turnout of candidates was recorded at recruitment camp. Altogether, 1254 youth attended the camp out of which 518 were from Kheda district. The analysis reveals that for 118 youth, the main source of information was television. For 100 youth, the source of information was teacher, sarpanch (village council head) and others. But for them television was the secondary source of information and it helped in confirming and reinforcing the message. Of course, remaining 300 were informed directly by Employment Exchange Officer. Awareness in terms of who can join army and the economic gains was observed amongst TV viewers not only by us but also by other Employment Exchange Officers, District Information Officer informed us that the TV viewers were better informed in terms of minimum requirements and physical standards. Taking clues from the interaction with the candidates, Recruiting Officer and Medical Officer of Army were contacted to find out corrective measures which were to be used as an input in the future programmes.

Television Support to Women Entrepreneur

Encouraged by the viewers' response, our second drive was for women entrepreneurs. Centre for Entrepreneurship Development (CED) invited women to avail the services of their Centre. We initiated programme production in this direction with the objective to : (a) emphasise on self-employment (b) inform the aspirant women regarding this scheme (c) motivate Kheda women to approach local branch of the organisation and (d) motivate the women viewers to avail to the training being imparted by CED.

The programme production approach for this purpose was informative and motivational. One quickie of 2.30 minites focussing on need, importance and avenues of self-employment for women was supported by announcements to join the classes. One documentary of 17 minutes informing about the procedure, duration, places and post-training prospects of self-employment was also produced and transmitted. After transmission 30 women approached CED. The TV viewers who produced CED were urban women. Since Kheda district was our experiment laboratory, we had asked CED project leader at Kheda to provide us feedback on our attempt.

Similar efforts were mounted to create awareness about the avenues open for self-employment of the youth.

Turning Point in Communication Strategy

Till 1983, television programmes were meant to support government efforts. In 1983, another need assessment study was conducted to find out how best their needs can be catered.

It was observed that there were 4,03,061 persons registered with Employment Office Kheda. Out of which 2,44,301 were literate and 1,58,760 were illiterate. The number of partially employed youth under Retention Allowance was not available. The prevalent belief was that higher the education better the employment chances. Economic situation being very complex at all the levels, at all the fronts, the youth accepted whatever job was offered to them. A kind of pessimism was quite obvious in their responses. Information to youth about various available careers (technical and non-technical) was very limited. The available information was vague, irrelevant, incomplete and untimely. Also the sources of information were very few and there was a lack of guidance for them.

At self-employment front, youth were found unaware of the existing government schemes for self-employment. They were worried about uncertainty of income. Fear of failure was the main constraint. Even if they decide to opt for self-employment, elderly persons seemed to prevent them and they did not know whom to contact. Corruption at various level were mentioned. Financial difficulties and marketing problems confused them. Some cases of cheating were also reported in the repayment of load instalments. Based on the study the problems were prioritized. Also a list of all the concerned Government, semi-Government and voluntary agencies dealing with the employment generation schemes was prepared. Employment Exchange Vocational Guidance Office, District Development Office, heads of all the Govern-ment agencies were contacted for getting information on self-employment schemes. All the available published literatures on 123 courses and 15 schemes were analysed. Selected beneficiaries (both successful and unsuccessful) of various schemes were interviewed. Based on these analysis it was decided to produce programmes with the objectives to: (a) inform about the various courses and schemes of self-employment (b) motivate youth to form cooperative societies as subsidy for such societies are higher (c) remove the fear of failure and encourage them to face the challenge and risk (d) narrate some success stories and highlight problems faced by the aspirant youth and (e) work as a link between the aspirant youth and the concerned official of the schemes.

Communication Approach

Informative, instructional, and motivational programmes were suggested to appeal youth to face the hurdles and succeed in achieving self-employment. Motivational approach was adopted to activate infra-structure including voluntary agencies. Guardians and parents were addressed by projecting failures as well as successes of each schemes.

Work is Welfare (Shram Ej Kalyan)

The work is welfare (Shram Ej Kalyan) serial was thought of in the initial stage in 1983. The format chosen was to intorduce scheme giving details about as to who can be benefitted, how much loan/subsidy can be given? Who should be approached? and what is the procedure. In the programme, salient features of the schemes were narrated by the concerned officials followed by the interviews of beneficiaries and the persons who have failed in getting the loan. In this series a Programme on Centre for Entrepreneurship Development was also produced. This programme covered training aspect of the institution alongwith the guidance. Programme on cottage industries were also produced. This was the beginnning of a new serial as a follow-up.

An attempt was made to assess the impact of this serial. To ascertain the gain in terms of knowledge, motivation and action, pre-telecast and post-telecast schedules were administered in two selected villages. The responses clearly indicated knowledge gains about procedure, contact place and training of various schemes. Further a number of letters were also received from the viewers seeking more details regarding the schemes. Analysis of viewers' letters provided several insights about the operational problems in the implementation of the programmes. Also some time officials responsible for these schemes reacted negatively to our efforts as it exposed some of the weakness of the schemes.

Employment Problems and Guidance (Rojgar Munjvan Ane Margadarshan)

Responses to "Work is Welfare" series brought many

problems to our notice. This series was in documentary and interview format, so it could not incorporate information regarding various technical and non-technical courses. Also SITE experiences had clearly indicated that programmes on development do not need sugar-coating of the messages. Since the viewers want these information in simple form, discussion format having informative and instructional approach was thought desirable.

Programme duration was decided for approximately 15 minutes. Before initaiting this serial we despatched a letter addressing to 280 youth clubs of Kheda District and villages having community television set inviting then to participate in our new serial in title (Rojgar Mujvan Ane Margadarshan). We repeatedly made announcements on televion asking youth to write to us their employment problems and the employment related information they want.Based on the replies we contacted the concerned officals and requested them to provide clear, complete and relevant replies. The researcher's role here was that of a "catalyst". This programme was produced in an informal coversational style wherein the viewers' letters depicting problems were read out and a concerned content expert answered the querries in detail. This programme serial was telecast in 68 parts. Atleast 560 letters were received from 49 locations ranging from the villages, small towns, and cities. Out of 560 letters, 399 came from urban viewers whereas 161 came from rural viewers. A clear difference was observed between rural viewers and urban viewers. While urban viewers sought information about higher study abroad, procedure for bank loan and issuing of character certificate the rural viewers sought educational and vocational guidance. Programme feedbacks were also obtained for this serial to further improve the utility of the programme.

Employment Guidance Camp (Rojgar Margadarshan Shibir)

Initial idea starting employment-oriented serials was to work as "information carrier" and also as a "guidance center."

"Link" Role

Our interest was not limited to transmitting information only. We also aimed at converting information in to action. To achieve this, we initiated to arrange "Employment Guidance Camps". To achieve this goal in selected villages, we analysed their employment problems, represented the problems to concerned officials and invited them to participate in camps to provide expertise help to the youth. In other words, it was an attempt to work as a "link" between the youth and the converned authority. The experiences were very interesting. We succeeded in arranging four such camps. We had invited all the concerned officers but only vocational guidance officers attended first camp, remaining officers gave one excuse or the other to avoid attending the camp.

In the first camp the response from the villagers was very disheartening We found the village inactive. The president and the members of the youth club were somewhat hesitant to participate in the camp.

One of the reasons for such a poor response was that the village elite did not want youth to take lead in organising any kind of function in the village. The village elite were in favour of **status quo**, while youth wanted their personal and professional development. The remaining three camps were well attended. The response from Government machinery also was positive. Almost all the officers who were invited turned up to participate. As intended, the dialogue between the youth and the officials was established. All the participants actively contributed and the youth expressed their grivances, and problems.

An average number of participants per camp was 90. The camp provided an excellent forum to exchange views and ideas of the youth. Our presence helped youth in being vocal and open while expressing their problems and their experiences with Employment Exchange Officer and other agencies. Another positive gain of these camps was that several youth actually got on the spot assistance in filling up loan applications, guidance and published literature on vocational courses, and employment opportunities. The participants for the first time verbalized their feelings and were able to express frankly and fearlessly. They also expressed satisfaction over officials' explanation. They commented that "this kind of camps can be more effective and useful, if more and more officers participate in the camp."

On the other hand, the participating officials also expressed their happiness as they got chace to face reality. They assured their support and co-operation for future camps. Use of television for providing face to face communiation was fruitful. Such camps have potentialities to cover viewers as well as non-viewers and arranging such camps indirectly enhance credibility of the television medium to some extend and its assistance in providing a participatory mode of information.

Light or Darkness (Andhkar Ke Ujas?)
Background: After a brief interval of eight months, (the time was consumed by research efforts) a new serial is launched

titled "Andhkar Ke Ujas?" A fresh attempt was made to assess youth needs.

Research Efforts: Since last four years experience made us familiar with the field reality. This time, we thought it better to involve Employment and Training Directorate from the very beginning. A committee was formed to plan out employment programmes. Main objectives were to suppot Government efforts like recruitment to armed forces, various self-employment schemes and also to make the Government aware of the people's problems. We wanted to bring the officials and the viewers together. We appealed to the viewers whether they would like to remain in darkness or would like to have bright future? We took enough care not to paint rosy picture in the employment field. We also portrayed difficulties in the field of self-employment.

Idea of involving Employment and Training Directorate was fruitful. We got overwhelming response from various corporations like Mahila Arthik Vikas Nigam, Backward Class Welfare Board, Minority Board, Cottage Industries etc. Employment and Training Directorate provided full support to our efforts. Director, Employment and Training himself appeared on screen for first two programmes. Response from the viewers was beyond our expectation. For the first month, 90 letters were received, and from the next month till now the monthly number is around 150. This programme includes answers to the letters, various Corporations schemes, exhibittions emphasising self-employment, vocational guidance, and direct competitive tests.

Till now 40 parts have been transmitted, each part is of about 12 to 14 minutes. It is an on-going series incorporating employment news.

A mid course evaluation study is also planned at the end of 52nd part.

Conclusion

"Andhkar Ke Ujas?" series is welcomed by all the agencies involved in the employment field. Previously, we had to rush from one office to anothor to find out useful, relevant and feasible information for our viewers. Now the table is turned. Concerned offices initiate and contact us and extend full co-operation in solving the problems which we represent for our viewers.

Few points become very obvious from our experience in the

field of employment-oriented programmes.

- It is the most relevant and useful programmes for the youth.
- Hardcore programme like employment do not need any entertaining formulas. Must be simple and direct.
- Programmes should not be more than 10-12 minutes or else it losses grip over the attention of the viewers.
- Language must be as simple as possible.
- Programme should not be content-loaded.
- Programme content should be supported by graphics.
- Recapitulation at the end of the programme should be done.
- Once heard may not be remembered, printed literature for followup is needed.
- Direct interaction of officials with the viewers increase compreshension.
- Priority should be given to low skilled cottage industries with low investment.
- Special programmes on women should be made for economic front
- Programme becomes more useful if it begins with employment news
- Everytime information sources and guidance sources shold be incorporated.
- Programme content should be supported with guickies and announcement to reinforce the message
- Periodical feedback and evaluation system should be evolved
- Viewers' exceptations and problems should be given more priority rather than government achievements.
- TV must be unbiased in representating viewers' problems. It should not work on the hypothesis that the viewer is always right.
- TV must insist on clear, complete and relevant answers from

the concerned officials.

- To increase viewers' involvement, letter-writers' names should be shown in the initial stages.

- TV viewers' efforts to follow programme's message should be appreciated and encouraged

FOOTNOTES

1. Kheda Communications Project (KCP) is run by Development and Educational Communications Unit of Indian Space Research Organization, Ahmedabad. It started alongwith Satellite Instructional Television Experiment (SITE) in 1975. KCP aimed at rural development. It transmitted programmes on agriculture, and health programmes related to economic and social change. The programmes are produced by a team which consists of producers, researchers, writers and subject experts. At present, the transmitter is located at Ahmedabad. It covers a range of 90 kms. radius encompassing 8 districts of Gujarat including Kheda district.

2. In this paper an attempt has been made to document the steps that were followed in converting the needs of the youth into television programmes. Also the feedback on the effects of these programmes on the Kheda youth were evaluated. The concept of youth used in this paper and in the actual studies and programme production relates to all those who are between the age-group of 15-24 years. The steps followed are: (a) needs assessment study, (b) identification of specific occupation for television support to create awareness, (c) programme production, (d) transmission - Feedback, with the help of viewers' letters and first-hand field visits during the programme transmission and follow-up activities as an activist. During the last six years, youth programmes thus produced and transmitted primarily made for rural youth are analysed here.

Binod C. Agrawal, Arbind Sinha, and Bela Trivedi

SELECTED BIBLIOGRAPHY ON SITE AND BEYOND SITE

In the following pages a selected bibliography has been presented. This bibliography is divided into four major sections. I. Before SITE researches; II. SITE researches; III. SITE continuity researches; and IV. General researches which contain a variety of articles. It has been updated taking into account the contributions of SITE and SITE continuity research team, mostly in the field of development and communication research.

SELECTED BIBLIOGRAPHY

PRE-SITE RESEARCHES

Anonymous

1969 Impact of Agricultural Television Programmes on Farmers in Delhi villages. Abstract of an Evaluation Report. New Delhi : Department of Adult Education, NCERT.

nd Impact of Film on Indian Society. New Delhi : AVID, Indian Space Research Organisation.

Chahil, Renu

1969 A Comparative Study of the Effectiveness of Radio, Television, and Pamphlets in the Communication of Agricultural and Family Planning Information. (Unpublished M.Sc. Thesis. New Delhi : Lady Irwin College.

Dey, P K

1968 Relative Effectiveness of Radio and Television as Mass Communication Media in Dissemination of

Agricultural Information. Unpublished M.Sc. Thesis. New Delhi : Indian Agricultural Research Institute.

Kaur, Ranbir

1970 Impact of Television on Farm Women. (Unpublished M.Sc. Thesis) New Delhi : Indian Agricultural Research Institute.

Lal, Chaman

1970 A Review of the Delhi Pilot Rural Television Project and its lessons. New Delhi : Indian Space Research Organisation.

1971 A Compilation of Questions asked by the Delhi Pilot Television Project (Krishi Darshan) Audiences. New Delhi : Indian Space Research Organisation.

Melzer, Alexander

1974 The Social use of India's Television Satellite : A Technology Assessment of the INSAT Proposal. Zurich: Centre for Economic Research, Swiss Federal Institute of Technology.

Sharma, S K and Jagdish Singh

1972 Television in Agricultural Transformation. New Delhi: Indian Council of Agricultural Research.

Sinha, B P

1974 Television in Diffusion of Farm Information. Delhi: New Heights.

Shingi, P M, and Bella Mody

1976 The Communication Effects Gap : A Field Experiment on Television and Agricultural Ignorance in India. **Communication Research,** Vol. 34 (2).

SITE RESEARCHES

SITE FORMATIVE

Aghi, Mira B
1975 How Research Can Improve Television Programmes.

Media Asia, 2 (1): 15-17.

1979 The Effectiveness of Science Education Programming. **Journal of Communication,** Vol. 29 (4): 104-105.

Agrawal, Binod C

1978 Anthropology and Satellite TV Communication in India. **The Anthropologist,** Vol. 22 (1 and 2) : 1-5.

Agrawal, Binod C assisted by J K Doshi

1974 Rajasthan Audience Profile. Ahmedabad: Space Applications Centre.

Agrawal, Binod C **et al.**

1974 a. SITE-Bihar Audience Profile. Ahmedabad : Space Application Centre.

1974 b. SITE-Madhya Pradesh (Chhattisgarh) Audience Profile. Ahmedabad : Space Applications Centre.

1974 c. SITE-Need Assessment Study - Kheda. Ahmedabad : Space Applications Centre.

1974 d. SITE-Orissa Audience Profile. Ahmedabad : Space Application Centre.

1974 e. SITE-Technical Report of Programme Pre-testing : Sandhana Dawda Quiz. Ahmedabad : Space Applications Centre.

Anonymous

1974 SITE Audience Profile: Kheda District-Gujarat. Ahmedabad: Space Applications Centre.

Bhaskaran, P

1975 SITE-Formative Research on SITE - Part I and II. Ahmedabad : Space Applications Centre.

Bhaskaran, P **et al.**

1974 SITE-Need Assessment Study : M.P. Ahmedabad : Space Applications Centre.

Doshi, J K **et al.**

1975 SITE-Needs Assessment Study - Bihar Cluster. Ahmedabad: Space Applications Centre.

Misra, R P and D P Pattanayak

1974 Audience Profile of Andhra Pradesh and Karnataka. Mysore: Central Institute of Indian Languages.

Mody, Bella

1974 SITE-Formative Research on SITE Part I and II. Ahmedabad: Space Applications Centre.

Mody, Bella, Prakash Suthar, and Rashida Rangwala

1977 Pre-testing Report Scripts 1, 3, 4 - Kheda Children's Self-Reliance Serial. Ahmedabad : Space Applications Centre.

Verma, K K

1974 SITE-Needs Assessment Study : Karnataka & Andhra Pradesh. Ahmedabad : Space Applications Centre.

1976 Needs Assessment Studies. In SITE Winter School Report. pp. 124-127. Ahmedabad : Space Applications Centre.

SITE PROCESS

Ahamed, S A

1977 A Study of the Role of Television Custodians in Community Viewing Situation of SITE. Paper presented in the meeting of Experts on SITE Evaluation at Department of Communication, Bangalore University, Bangalore, April 20-22, 1977.

Bhatia, B S

1977 a. SITE-Programme Assessment by Field Experts. Ahmedabad : Space Applications Centre.

1977 b. SITE-TV set Performance. Ahmedabad : Space Applications Centre.

Bhatia, B S, D R Wakharikar and P K Joshi

nd Kheda TV Operation: A Spot Study. Ahmedabad : Space Applications Centre.

Bhaskaran, P

1976 Feedback System for SITE. In SITE Winter School Report, pp. 139-151. Ahmedabad : Space Applications Centre.

Bhaskaran, P assisted by Ila Patel

1977 a. SITE : Evening Feedback. Ahmedabad : Space Applications Centre.

1977 b. SITE for children : Morning Feedback. Ahmedabad: Space Applications Centre.

Karnik, K S

1977 Pij Transmission : A Quantitative Analysis. Ahmedabad: Space Applications Centre.

Mody, Bella

1977 SITE Message System Analysis. Ahmedabad : Space Applications Centre.

1979 Programming for SITE. **Journal of Communication.** Vol. 29 (4) : 90-98.

Mody, Bella and Rashida Rangwala

1975 Kheda Lab Report for Production Cell - Harijans and God. Ahmedabad : Space Applications Centre.

1977 Kheda Lab Report for Production Cell - Balmike's **Sha Maatey.** Ahmedabad : Space Applications Centre.

Mody, Bella with Dalpat Sarupria

1977 SITE Message Systems Analysis - What did SITE Programmes consist of? Ahmedabad : Space Applications Centre.

1975 SITE in Sight. Ahmedabad : Space Applications

Centre.

SITE SUMMATIVE

Aghi, Mira B

1977 a. SITE-Baseline Report : Science Education Programmes. Ahmedabad: Space Applications Centre.

1977 b. Impact of Science Education Programmes on SITE Children of Rajasthan. Ahmedabad : Space Applications Centre.

Agrawal, Binod C

1976 a. Holistic Studies : An Anthropological Approach for Evaluating SITE. In SITE Winter School Report, pp: 165-171. Ahmedabad : Space Applications Centre.

1976 b. Media, Anthropology and Rural Development : Some Observations on SITE. Ahmedabad : Space Applications Centre.

1977 a. Media Research and Anthropology : Some Observations on SITE. In Evaluating Educational Television and Radio, (eds.) Tony Bates and John Robinson : pp. 285-287. Milton Keynes : The Open University Press.

1977 b. Satellite Instructional Television Experiment : A Social Evaluation. In Evaluating Educational Television and Radio, (eds.) Tony Bates and John Robinson : pp. 122-125. Milton Keynes : The Open University Press.

1978 Television Comes to Village : An Evaluation of SITE. Bangalore : Indian Space Research Organisation.

1979 SITE Social Evaluation : Results and Research Experiences. Ahmedabad : Space Applications Centre.

1981 a. SITE Social Evaluation : Results, Experiences and Implications. Ahmedabad : Space Applications Centre.

1981 b. Anthropological Applications in Communication Research and Evaluation of SITE in India. **Media Asia,** Vol. 8 (3) pp. 136-146.

Agrawal, Binod C, J K Doshi, K K Verma and V Jesudasan

1977 Social Impact of SITE on adults (Part I & II). Bangalore: Indian Space Research Organisation.

Agrawal, Binod C and J B Ambekar

1979 Inducing Change Through Television : An Evaluative Study of SITE in a Karnataka Village. Ahmedabad : Space Applications Centre.

Agrawal, Binod C and Kumkum Rai

1980 Women, Television and Rural Development : An Evaluative Study of SITE in a Rajasthan Village. Ahmedabad : Space Applications Centre.

Agrawal, Binod C and Arbind K Sinha

1981 Satellite Television in a Bihar Village : A Case Study of SITE. Ahmedabad : Space Applications Centre.

Agrawal, Binod C and M R Malek

1985 Television in Kheda : A Social Evaluation of SITE. New Delhi : Concept Publishing Company.

Ambekar, J B

1980 Channels of Communication and Development in a Rural Community. (unpublished Ph. D. thesis) Dharwad : Karnataka University

Anonymous

nd Satellite Instructional Television Experiment : An Evaluation of its Social Impact. New Delhi : Planning Commission.

1981 Evaluation Report on Satellite Instructional Television Experiment. New Delhi : Planning Commission.

Bashiruddin, S

1977 SITE Experiences of National Institute for Community Development : An Overview. Paper presented in SITE Evaluation Seminar (Karnataka Cluster). Bangalore : Bangalore University.

Bhaskaran, K S V Reddy, and B V Sundershah Rao

1977 Farm Training Through 'SITE' (An Experimental Study in Andhra Pradesh). Paper presented in the Regional Seminar on Strategy of Rural TV Research Convened by NICD-ICSSR, Hyderabad on September 12-13, 1977.

Bhatia, B S with Ajay Chauhan

1977 Satellite Instructional Television Experiment - Media Utilization. Bangalore : Indian Space Research Organisation.

Chakravarty, T K and H P Arya

1977 Evaluation Studies on Community Forums - Some Methodological Considerations. Paper for NICD-ICSSR Regional Seminar on Strategy of Rural Television Research September 12-13, 1977.

Chauhan, K N K and B P Sinha

1976 Impact of SITE on Adoption of Farm Technology. **Indian Journal of Extension Education**, Vol. XII (3 & 4): 14-21.

1977 Effects of SITE TV on Democratic-Conservative Outlook of the Rural Audience. **Indian Journal of Extension Education**, Vol. XIII (1 & 2) : 9-14.

1979 Impact of SITE Television on the Audiences' Efficacy and Faith in Norms. **Indian Journal of Extension Education**, Vol. XV (3 & 4) : 15-21.

Chitnis, E V

1977 Preface. **In Social Impact** of SITE on Adults by Binod C Agrawal **et al.** Ahmedabad : Space Applications Centre.

Dighe, Anita and Prodipto Roy

1977 Factors Affecting Comprehension and Retension of Selected SITE Programmes. New Delhi : Council for Social Development.

1978 Social Impact of Television on Rural Adult of Kheda (Gujarat). Ahmedabad : Space Applications Centre.

Eapen, K E

1979 The Cultural Component of SITE. **Journal of Communication**, 29 (4) : 106-113.

Gore, M S

1979 A Critical Assessment of the Studies relating to the Satellite Instructional Television Experiment. Bombay: Tata Institute of Social Sciences.

1979 The Satellite Instructional Television Experiment (SITE). **Society and Science** Vol. 2 (4).

Karnik, Kiran

1981 Development Television in India. **Educational Broadcasting International.** September 1981 : 131-135.

Karnik, K S and N Sampath (eds.)

1977 UN-UNESCO panel meeting on SITE Experiences. Ahmedabad : Space Applications Centre.

Mrutyunjayam N, and T Somasundaram

1977 Viewing Behaviour and Farmers' Preference to the Subject Matter of Agriculture Telecast through SITE in Hyderabad District. Paper for Regional Seminar on Strategy of Rural TV Research Convened by NICD-ICSSR, Hyderabad September 12-13, 1977.

Neurath, Paul

nd School Television in Delhi. New Delhi : All India Radio.

Pal, Yash

1978 The Singular Success of SITE. How Satellite can Teach Indian Villages by Television. **Science Review** 3 (1) : 55-57.

Rahman, Saulat

nd SITE-Educational Television : An Exploratory Study of Educational Satellite Broadcast Television Programme in Orissa. New Delhi : Ministry of Education and Social Welfare.

Ramadasmorthy, V D, Hanumantha Rao

1978 Nutrition Education and SITE Telecasts. **International Journal of Health Education,** Vol. 21 : 168-173.

Rao, B S S

1980 Television for Rural Development (A Study in Maharashtra). (unpublished Ph.D thesis). Pune : University of Poona.

Sachchidananda, and M N Jha

1980 Communication in a Bihar Village : An Evaluation of SITE. Ahmedabad : Space Applications Centre.

Sachchidananda and K K Pandey

1980 SITE Evaluation Through Holistic Study - Bhutera (Rajasthan). Ahmedabad : Space Applications Centre.

Sanjay, B P

1977 An Evaluation of the Multi-Media Package Programme for Teacher Training in SITE. A paper presented in the Meeting of Experts in SITE Evaluation at Department of Communication. Bangalore University, Bangalore April 20-22, 1977.

Satish Chandra, B R

1977 Analysis of the TV-Behaviour of User and Non-user Teachers in Relation to Teleschool Programme:

A Comparative study in Karnataka Cluster of SITE. A paper presented in the meeting of Experts on SITE Evaluation at Department of Communications. Bangalore University, Bangalore. April 20-22, 1977.

Schramm, Wilbur

1976 What do we know about SITE? Paper presented in the study Seminar on SITE, November 8-12 1976 at Ahmedabad.

Shanmugam, A V and Leela Rao

1977 Meeting of Experts on SITE Evaluation (Bangalore : 20-22, April, 1977). Bangalore: Department of Communication, Bangalore University.

Shingi, P M, G Kaur and R P Rai

1982 Television and Knowledge-Gap Hypothesis. Ahmedabad: Indian Institute of Management.

Shukla, Snehlata

1979 The Impact of SITE on Primary School Children. **Journal of Communication**, Vol. 29 (4) : 99-105.

Shukla, Snehlata and Kuldip Kumar

1977 SITE-Impact of SITE on Primary School Children. Bangalore : Indian Space Research Organisation.

Sinha, Arbind K

1977 Conclusion and Implications of Holistic Studies and Social Impact of SITE on Adults (with Binod C Agrawal). Paper presented in UN-UNESCO panel meeting on SITE experiences, Ahmedabad.

1978 Role of Satellite Communication in Rural Development. Paper present in 4th Annual Conference of Ethnographic and Folk Culture Society, U.P.

1985 **Role of Mass Media in Rural Development : A Study of Village Communication in Bihar.** New Delhi : Concept Publishing Company.

Sondhi, Krishan

nd An Approach to the Indian Satellite Television Project : A Study in Communication and Culture (unpublished paper).

Sondhi, Krishan (ed.)

nd Satellite Communication and Family Planning. New Delhi : Audio Visual Instructional Division, ISRO.

Trehan, Vijay R.

1979 A Study of Social Effects of Withdrawal of Television from the Satellite Instructional Television Experiment (SITE) Villages in India. (unpublished Master thesis). University of Hawaii.

Umaddin, K.

1977 An Evaluation of Multi-Media Training for Extension Workers and Farmers. A paper presented in the meeting of experts on SITE Evaluation at Department of Communication. Bangalore University, Bangalore : April 20-22, 1977.

SITE CONTINUITY

Anonymous

nd A Brief Report on Impact Study undertaken in the SITE Continuity Clusters of Jaipur and Raipur. Ahmedabad : Space Applications Centre.

1978 Kheda TV - Impact Study. Ahmedabad : Space Applications Centre.

1979 Research for Television Programmes - Kheda Experiences. Ahmedabad : Space Applications Centre.

1981 A Study of Programmes of Doordarshan Pij - Ahmedabad (Observations and Depth Interviews). Delhi: Audience Research Unit, Doordarshan Kendra.

Bruce, Cecilia

1985 A Bird's Eye-view of Ahmedabad-Pij TV

programmes. Ahmedabad : Development and Educational Communication Unit.

Dighe, Anita

1977 Agricultural labourers in Jaipur District - A Study of their Needs and Problems. New Delhi : Council for Social Development.

Joshi, Hansa

1984 NTV : Sanshudhan Nu Darshtikon (in Gujarati). Ahmedabad : Development and Educational Communication Unit.

1985 a. Bhadake Bole Chhe Zindagi (in Gujarati) Ahmedabad: Development and Educational Communication Unit.

1985 b. Visami Sadiman Strivikas (in Gujarati). Ahmedabad: Development and Educational Communication Unit.

Joshi, Hansa, and S R Joshi

1982 Adult Education in Villages - A Study. Ahmedabad: Space Applications Centre.

Joshi, S R

1977 Kheda TV Operation Study. Ahmedabad : Space Applications Centre.

1983 a. Community Viewing : The Need and the Problem. **Social Change** 13 (3) : 40-44.

1983 b. Gatekeepers at Receiving End. Ahmedabad : Space Applications Centre.

1983 c. Reflections on a Workshop with Badal Sircar, Vishrampura, Kheda. Ahmedabad : Space Applications Centre.

1983 d. Feature films on TV? Ahmedabad : Space Applications Centre.

1983 e. What went on air? Ahmedabad : Space Applications Centre.

Joshi, S R, and Ila Patel

1978 How News is Received - Recomendations to make it More Effective. Ahmedabad : Space Applications Centre.

Joshi, S R, Neela Trivedi and Anil Patel

1978 Pretesting Prototype Programmes (Manra Manra Pher). Ahmedabad : Space Applications Centre.

Misra, Radha

1984 Images and Messages. Ahmedabad : Development and Educational Communication Unit.

1985 Children's Programmes : What's in it? Ahmedabad: Development and Educational Communication Unit.

Misra, Radha et al.

1983 Towards Educational Programming for Children : A Report. Ahmedabad : Space Applications Centre.

Misra, Radha, Hansa Joshi and K M Parmar

1983 Formal Education Programmes Impact Study. Ahmedabad: Space Applications Centre.

Parmar, K M, et al.

1980 A Study of Special Transmission for Seventh Lok Sabha Election Results, 1980. Ahmedabad : Space Applications Centre.

Patel, Anil

1978 a. A Study of the Valod Taluka Development Experiment. Ahmedabad : Space Applications Centre.

1978 b. Farmer's Cooperative Society of Gambhira. Ahmedabad: Space Applications Centre.

Patel, Ila

1978 a. Kheda Audience Composition Study. Ahmedabad: Space Applications Centre.

1978 b. Needs Assessment Study of Kheda Children (Grade I and II). Ahmedabad : Space Applications Centre.

1978 c. Pretesting Prototype Programme (Laxman Rekha). Ahmedabad : Space Applications Centre.

Patra, Swarupananda

1978 Social Change/Education : Its Dynamics, Need Assessments, Programme Briefs, Strategies and Instructional Objectives. Ahmedabad : Space Applications Centre.

Rajasekhara, Reddy G, and B Subramanyam

1978 Impact Study - Hyderabad Services Zone, Ahmedabad: Space Applications Centre.

Rangwala, Rasheeda

1980 Formative Study on Scabies and Impact of its Programmes. Ahmedabad : Space Applications Centre.

Rangwala, Rasheeda, Ila Patel and Bella Mody

1977 The Economics of Good Health : A TV Strategy for the Kheda Monsoons. Ahmedabad : Space Applications Centre.

Shah, Manjari

1983 Pretesting of Non-Verbal Programmes. Ahmedabad: Space Applications Centre.

1984 The Second Channel of Ahmedabad. Ahmedabad : Development and Educational Communication Unit.

1985 Kheda : Health. Ahmedabad : Development and Educational Communication Unit.

Shah, Manjari and K M Parmar

1982 The Impact of Asiad Transmission on Kheda TV Operation. Ahmedabad : Space Applications Centre.

Shah, Manjari, Hansa Joshi and K M Parmar

1984 The Option of Channels and the Ahmedabad

Viewers. Ahmedabad : Space Applications Centre.

Shah, Renuka

1977 Predominant Caste/Group, Population and Census Book. Location Code of TV Villages in Kheda District. Ahmedabad : Space Applications Centre.

nd Report on Pretesting of a Programme in a New Format. Ahmedabad : Space Applications Centre.

Singh, Jagdish

1983 - A Report on Quick Feedback obtained from the User-Teacher on ETV Programmes in Andhra Pradesh and Orissa. New Delhi : National Council for Educational Research and Training.

Sinha, Arbind K

1981 -SITE Village Re-visited. Ahmedabad : Space Applications Centre.

Srivastava, Gayatri

1981 Audience Information, Need Assessment and Research Utilization for ETV Programming in the Indian Kheda Communication Project. (unpublished M.Sc. thesis) Manila University of Philippines.

Trivedi, Bela

1983 Where is Employment? Ahmedabad: Space Applications Centre.

1984 Reactions and Suggestions on Kakani Deli. Ahmedabad: Development and Educational Communication Unit.

1984 Glimpses of Field Laboratory. Ahmedabad: Development and Educational Communication Unit.

1985 TV : A New Dimension in Political Awareness? Ahmedabad: Development and Educational Communication Unit.

1986 Andhkar Ke Ujas (in Gujarati). Ahmedabad : Development and Educational Communication Unit.

1986 Viewership Survey. Ahmedabad : Development and Educational Communication Unit.

Trivedi, Bela, K M Parmar and Anil Patel

nd A Study of Audience Reactions to Doordarshan Programmes. Ahmedabad : Space Applications Centre.

GENERAL

Agrawal, Binod C

1976 Some Observations on the Rural Child in India. In "The Child and the Community" Indian Association for Preschool Education (1976).

1980 SITE Mid-Way : An Evaluative Study of Nine Villages. Ahmedabad : Space Applications Centre.

1982 a. Satellite Communication Technology for Development: The Indian Scene. Paper presented in the International Association for Mass Communication Research held at Paris, September 6-10, 1982.

1982 b. Communication's Structures in India: A Case Study of Television. Paper presented in the International Association for Mass Communication Research, held at Paris, September 6-10, 1982.

1983 a. Can Media be Friend of Poof? Socio-Political Implications of Communication Technologies in India **Media Development**, Vol. 30 (4) : 26-38.

1983 b. Instructional Television for Rural Women : Some Observations from Kheda (with Arbind K Sinha). Vidura.

1983 c. Anthropology in India : Some Reflections. Paper presented in the Seminar on "Modernization of Teaching and Research in Anthropology. Delhi University, February, 1983.

1984 a. Reflection on Communication Research for Development in India. Paper presented in the National Seminar on Communication for Development, New Delhi, February 1-4, 1984.

1984 b. Social Implications of New Communication Technologies in India. Paper presented in the National Seminar on Communication for Development, New Delhi, February 1-4, 1984.

1984 c. Need for Action Research in Communication : A Case Study of the Yanadi Tribe in India. Paper presented in the National Seminar on Communication for Development, New Delhi. February 1-4, 1984.

1984 d. Technological Vector of Video Cassette Recorders in the Cultural Context of India. Paper presented in 14th IAMCR conference, Prague, Czechoslovakia, August 27-31, 1984.

1984 e. Communication Research related to Women and Children. Paper presented in ICCTR-UNICEF Seminar on 'Media Utilization for the Development of Women and Children', New Delhi, September 11-12, 1984.

1984 f. A Decade of Communication Research : Some Reflection for the Future. Paper presented in ISRO-UNICEF seminar on SITE-INSAT : Production of Programmes for Women and Children, Ahmedabad, November 26-28, 1984.

Baradi, H J

1978 No Prescriptions Please : **Seminar 232** : 33-35.

Block, Clifford, Dennis R Foote and John K Mayo

1979 SITE Unseen : Implications for Programming and Policy. **Journal of Communication.** Vol. 1.29 (4): 114-124.

Chander, Ramesh and Kiran Karnik

1976 Planning for Satellite Broadcasting : The Indian Instructional Television Experiment. UNESCO. Reports and papers on Mass Communication No. 78.

Chitnis, E V

1974 a. Satellite Television. Ahmedabad : Space Applications Centre.

1974 b. Satellite Instructional Television Experiment, paper No. 6. Seminar for Key Administrators. Ahmedabad: Space Applications Centre.

1975 Some Practical Aspects of Satellite Communication. Ahmedabad : Space Applications Centre.

1976 a. Introduction to SITE. In SITE Winter School, January 16-28, 1976 pp. : 5-16. Ahmedabad : Space Applications Centre.

1976 b. Social Implications of the Satellite Instructional Television Experiment - The Use of an Advanced Satellite Communication System for National Development. Ahmedabad Space Applications Centre.

1978 Participatory Software. Seminar 232 : 22-27.

Doshi, J K

1977 Communication : Breaking New Path in Anthropology. Ahmedabad ; Space Applications Centre.

Joshi, P G

1978 Implications of India/U.S. Instructional Television Satellite Experiment Project (SITE).

Joshi, S R

1976 Mode of Operation. Seminar 232: 36-37.

Karnik, K S

1977 Motivation in Projects : Lessons from SITE. Ahmedabad: Space Applications Centre.

1978 Organisational Structure, Working Culture and Value systems. Paper presented at Xth International Congress of Anthropological and Ethnological Sciences. Delhi: December 1978.

Mody, Bella

1978 Lessons from the Indian Satellite Experiment. Educational Broadcasting International 2 September.

Mohanty, B B

1977 Satellite Instructional Television Experiments. Washington, D.C., Association for Educational Communication and Technology.

Pal, Yash

1978 The Crucial Decision. **Seminar 232**: 12-15.

1979 When will Space Lead to Development? Ahmedabad: Space Applications Centre.

Shroff, A A

1976 SITE : Software Aspect. **In** SITE Winter School January 16-28, 1976. pp: 83-96. Ahmedabad : Space Applications Centre.

Sinha, Arbind K

1978 Anthropology in Visual Communication. Paper presented in the Symposium of Visual Anthropology. Xth International Congress of Anthropology and Ethnographical Sciences, December 1978 at New Delhi.

1981 Action Anthropology : A Challenge for Development. Paper presented in the 7th Ethnographic and Folk Culture Society meeting held at Bidisa (W.B).

1982 a. Communication in Gujarat - 1981 Cyclone (with Shirish Avrani). **Disaster** Vol. 8 (1): 67-73.

1982 b. First day of Colour TV : An Analysis from Pij (Co-author) Ahmedabad : Space Applications Centre.

1983 a. Human Response to Disaster Communication : An Analysis of Amreli - Gandhinagar APPLE Link (Co-author). Ahmedabad : Space Applications Centre.

1983 b. The Problems of Development : Some Reflections from SUNCom-82. Ahmedabad : Space Applications Centre.

1983 c. Agriculture and Weather Forecasting : An Analysis of Unseasonal Rains in Delhi during April 1983

(Co-author). Ahmedabad : Space Applications Centre.

Space Applications Centre

1979 INSAT Utilization for Education and Development : A System Study. Ahmedabad : Space Applications Centre.

Taher, Naznin

1976 Production of SITE Science Education Programmes : A Study in Communication (unpublished M.Sc. Thesis). Bangalore : Department of Communication, Bangalore University.

Vishwanath, K

1978 Case Studies. **Seminar** 232: 28-32.

Anonymous

1974 SITE-Proceedings of the SITE Social Research Seminar, May 13-14, 1974.

1974 Software Research Plan for Satellite Instructional Television Experiment (A proposal) Pantnagar : G B Pant University of Agriculture and Technology.

1974 Software Research Plan for Satellite Instructional Television Experiment (A proposal) Pantnagar : G B Pant University of Agriculture and Technology.

1975 SITE Social Evaluation Operation Plan. Ahmedabad : Space Applications Centre.

1976 SITE Winter School, January 16-28, 1976. Ahmedabad Space Applications Centre.

1976 Seminar on "Satellite Communication and Anthropology". Lucknow, January 27-29, 1976. Ahmedabad : Space Applications Centre.

1976 SITE Proceedings of Study Seminar on SITE-Evaluation November 8-12, 1976. Ahmedabad : Space Applications Centre.

1976 SITE-Seminar on "Satellite Communication and

Anthropology" Lucknow January 27-29, 1976.

1976 Proceedings of Study Seminar on SITE Evaluation. November 8-12, 1976. Ahmedabad : Space Applications Centre.

1976 On SITE in India. A Report of the Commonwealth study visit to India's SITE Experiment April 4-17, 1976. Commonwealth Secretariat, Commonwealth Braodcasting Association.

nd Report of the Seminar of Key Administrators on Systems Approach to SITE. New Delhi : NCERT

INDEX